Codes and Masks

Mária Kurdi

Codes and Masks

Aspects of Identity in Contemporary Irish Plays in an Intercultural Context

PETER LANG

Frankfurt am Main · Berlin · Bern · Bruxelles · New York · Oxford · Wien

Die Deutsche Bibliothek - CIP-Einheitsaufnahme

Kurdi, Mária:

Codes and masks : aspects of identity in contemporary Irish plays in an intercultural context / Mária Kurdi. - Frankfurt am Main ; Berlin ; Bern ; Bruxelles ; New York ; Oxford ; Wien : Lang, 2000
    ISBN 3-631-35972-1

ISBN 3-631-35972-1
US-ISBN 0-8204-4723-4

© Peter Lang GmbH
Europäischer Verlag der Wissenschaften
Frankfurt am Main 2000
All rights reserved.

Printed in Germany 1 2   4 5 6 7

To the memory of my father,
Mihály Kurdi (Wien 1916 – Sopron 1951)

Acknowledgements

This book is published with the financial assistance of the Hungarian National Scholarly and Scientific Research Fund (OTKA), as part of a grant under the contract number T 023 480. The writing of five out of the ten essays included here was supported by the same fund, namely "Historical Fragmentation Impacting National Identity: A Postcolonial Reading of Thomas Murphy's *Famine*"; "'Ireland mustn't be such a bad place, so, if the Yanks want to come here to do their filming.' Reflections on the West and Irishness in Martin McDonagh's Plays"; "Alternative Articulations of Female Subjectivity and Gender Relations in Contemporary Irish Women's Plays: the Example of Marina Carr"; "New Strangers in the House? Immigrants and Natives in Donal O'Kelly's *Asylum! Asylum!* and John Barrett's *Borrowed Robes*"; "Romanticism, Identity and Intertextuality: Edmund Burke in Late Twentieth Century Irish Criticism and Drama."

All the ten essays have been published in other collections or journals already. Herewith, I gratefully acknowledge the respective editors' and publishers' permission to reprint edited versions of the following copyrighted material:

"Historical Fragmentation Impacting National Identity: A Postcolonial Reading of Thomas Murphy's *Famine*" from Tamás Bényei and Péter Szaffkó (eds.), *Happy Returns: Essays for István Pálffy* (Debrecen: KLU, Institute of English and American Studies, 1999)

"Cycling Pairs and Doubles in a House Divided Against Itself: Stewart Parker's *Spokesong*" as the expanded and retitled version of "The Ways of Twoness: Pairs, Parallels and Contrasts in Stewart Parker's *Spokesong*" from Donald E. Morse, Csilla Bertha and István Pálffy (eds.), *A Small Nation's Contribution to the World: Essays on Anglo-Irish Literature and Language* (Debrecen: Kossuth Lajos University, 1993; Gerrards Cross: Colin Smythe, 1993)

"'Ireland mustn't be such a bad place, so, if the Yanks want to come here to do their filming': Reflections on the West and Irishness in Martin McDonagh's Plays" from Shawn O'Hare (ed.), *Nua* 3.1 (Autumn 1999)

"Alternative Articulations of Female Subjectivity and Gender Relations in Contemporary Irish Women's Plays: the Example of Marina Carr" from László Ferenczi and Lóránt Kabdebó (eds.), *Irodalomtudomány* 1.2 (Autumn 1999)

"Female Self-Cure Through Revisioning and Refashioning Male/Master Narratives in Anne Devlin's *After Easter*" from Zoltán Abádi-Nagy (ed.), *The Hungarian Journal of English and American Studies: Irish Drama Issue* 2.2 (Autumn 1996)

"New Strangers in the House? Immigrants and Natives in Donal O'Kelly's *Asylum! Asylum!* and John Barrett's *Borrowed Robes*" from Zoltán Abádi Nagy (ed.), *The Hungarian Journal of English and American Studies: Special Issue on Contemporary Irish Literature in Honour of Brian Friel at 70* 5.1 (Spring 1999)

"Romanticism, Identity and Intertextuality: Edmund Burke in Late Twentieth Century Irish Criticism and Drama" from Éva Bús, Imre Garaczi and Zoltán Kalmár (eds.), *Carmen Saeculare VII. "Glowing Hours"* (Veszprém: University of Veszprém, 1999)

"'We all have our codes. We all have our masks': Language and Politics in Brian Friel's Stage Version of *Fathers and Sons*" from C. C. Barfoot and Rias van den Doel (eds.), *Ritual Remembering: History, Myth and Politics in Anglo-Irish Drama. Proceedings of the Leiden IASAIL Conference: Volume 2* (Amsterdam—Atlanta, GA,1995)

"Rewriting the Reread: Brian Friel's Version of Turgenev's *A Month in the Country*" from Anthony Roche (ed.), *Irish University Review* 25.2 (Autumn/ Winter 1995)

"Brian Friel and American Drama" from György Novák (ed.), *HUSSE Papers 1995. Proceedings of the Second Conference of HUSSE* (Szeged: Attila József University, 1995).

Contents

Introduction

The present collection comprises ten essays which engage in analysing the variety of ways the complex issue of identity is explored in some contemporary Irish plays. They were conceived over the period of 1994-1999, with one of them, about Stewart Parker's *Spokesong*, being an expanded, rearranged and retitled version of a 1993 original. Together, they do not seek to be representative of the whole bulk of drama written in and about Ireland since the 1960s, yet undertake highlighting and contextualising meaningful occurrences of a particular cluster of themes and corresponding strategies within it.

The phrase "Codes and Masks" in the main title of the volume derives from Brian Friel's adaptation of Turgenev's *Fathers and Sons*, where one of the protagonists asserts that "We all have our codes. We all have our masks." This can be found emblematic of the multifaceted issue of identity and its artistic manifestations, which have been central to the drama of Ireland in the last a hundred years or more. It was the pronounced need for national self-definition that gave life to the genre, and compelled Irish playwrights to experiment with forms and styles that would invest their works with an identity distinct from mainstream English literature. In the postcolonial era the issue appears as pertinent as ever, drawing on experiences which reflect how the historically, socially as well as culturally grounded dialogue with themselves and with others both influences and shapes the identity concepts of the Irish and the aesthetic qualities informing their drama. Since self-constitution is understood as a discursive process, "aspects of identity" as a subject calls for being perceived within the matrix of a continuous, protean interweave of language and other cultural forces, which appear as thematic strands in individual works.

The essays are arranged into three parts which discuss respective authors and plays, addressing questions of national and communal, individual and gender identity and the identity of dramatic works. No rigid boundary, however, is supposed to exist between these areas, bearing in mind the subtle interrelations of the individual, society and drama itself. In part one, Thomas Murphy's *Famine* and Stewart Parker's *Spokesong* are analysed, focusing on their dramatisation of the interplay between history and politics, the dynamics of place and identity. These essays also treat ways of applying the Brechtian technique of distancing to the Irish stage, and also how drama can convey a sense of ambiguity and doubling through its self-conscious mixture of theatrical modes. This part of the volume is completed by a discussion of Martin McDonagh's first four works, pointing out that they reshape as well as deconstruct elements of Synge's anti-colonial drama and develop a strategy that fuses the postcolonial and the postmodern. What McDonagh's drama constitutes, in this interpretation, is a possible world involving undesirable conditions as a negative alternative, to exorcise the demons of inherited distortions and to expose the alienating effects of the globalising, media-ruled present.

Having emerged as a ramifying subject recently, the issue of gender can be seen as firmly rooted in the history and culture of Ireland. In the second part of the book, the essays dealing with the works of Marina Carr and Anne Devlin probe into their reflections on the changing pattern of gender relations and on women's chances for self-fulfilment. Both playwrights are found to be re-reading the forms and conventions of drama created by male authors. In Carr's case the inclusion of special devices of the fantastic is highlighted, while Devlin's *After Easter* qualifies as an integrative play that revisions patriarchal narratives from a female angle. Following them, the third essay is inspired by the very timely subject of how the Irish respond to the phenomenon of intensifying immigration into their country, underscoring the dialectical relationship between the variety of personal attitudes to the dislocation of the foreign other and the problems it brings to the surface in the host community. The two plays examined together are constructed around real events: Donal O'Kelly's *Asylum! Asylum!* reaches back to an incident reported from Northern Uganda, whereas John Barrett's *Borrowed Robes* uses the context of the 1904 Limerick pogrom against local Jews. Coming last in the second part of the collection, the essay titled "Romanticism, Identity and Intertextuality: Edmund Burke in Late Twentieth Century Irish Criticism and Drama" embodies a kind of borderline case, in that it marks a transition to the final group. Underpinned by the processes of recanonisation in contemporary Irish criticial discourse, it surveys the intertextual presence of Burke in Brian Friel's *Philadelphia, Here I Come!* and Thomas Kilroy's *Double Cross*.

The book closes with three essays that address some plays by Brian Friel. His stage versions of Turgenev's *Fathers and Sons* and *A Month in the Country* are viewed in their connection with the playwright's other work, foregrounding the aesthetic aspects of identity. The former is discussed as a "language play," and the analysis of *A Month in the Country* builds on receptionist theory, indicating the role of the audience in realising the potential of the work. Comparative in focus, the last essay, "Brian Friel and American Drama," traces parallels of theme and technique rather than influence, suggesting that the identity of plays is profoundly affected by their implicit conversation with several other pieces of world drama. In spite of their divergent routes, Irish and American drama have been linked by their unfailing interest in the vigorous interpenetration of public and private constraints. Commented on at some length, the discussion includes parallels and differences between Friel's postmodern *Faith Healer* and its American counterpart, William V. Moody's *The Faith Healer* from the turn of the century.

The "intercultural context" mentioned in the subtitle of the volume refers to the method of inquiry adopted here in the broadest possible sense. In addition to drawing widely on the recent results of Irish scholarship, the essays deploy a choice of perspectives developed in international criticism, applying elements of postcolonial, cultural materialist, feminist and receptionist theories. Throughout, there is a tendency to describe affinities and contrasts with the classics of Irish drama as well as with world theatre, including authors like Edward Albee, Samuel Beckett, Caryl Churchill, Henrik Ibsen, Arthur Miller, Sam Shepard, Tennessee Williams and W. B. Yeats, reinforcing the notion that contemporary Irish drama does not flourish in isolation. Intertextuality, rewriting, adaptation and examples for the palimpsest also come under scrutiny, to elucidate a trend discovered to be increasingly significant in our time.

Finally, I hope that my position as an informed outsider to Irish culture also contributes to the scope and depth of the investigation the book presents. Considering the evidence of some commonality of experience, Hungary is but another country challenged to develop new approaches to the question of identity in both life and literature. Through its intellectual and artistic richness, contemporary Irish drama holds a mirror up to the concerns of more than one nation.

Part One

National and Communal Identity

Historical Fragmentation Impacting National Identity: A Postcolonial Reading of Thomas Murphy's *Famine*

Introduction

Reacting to the conspicuous absence of Ireland from most theorisations of the postcolonial until quite recently, Luke Gibbons writes that the conquest of the country established there "the classical colonial patterns," bringing "an entire nation to the brink of catastrophe, with the occurrence of the Great Famine in the mid-nineteenth century."[1] Unarguably, the Famine marks a period of devastating events and effects in the history of Ireland. Involving human loss on a vast scale and incurring dramatic changes in the structure of the population's life, it also had a considerable part in the re-formation of national consciousness and identity. During the years of 1845-49 and their aftermath about a million people died of starvation or various famine-related diseases, and an even greater number chose or were forced to choose emigration.[2] It is hardly a wonder that the memory of the Famine has been haunting the nation's folk traditions and literature down to our times. Writing about farming activities, Seamus Heaney's poem "At a Potato Digging" flashes up this ineradicable feature of the Irish historical experience, its continuity stressed by words like "still" and "running." Painful self-searching of comparable magnitude informs the Protestant John Hewitt's poem "The Scar," in which the speaker claims to have been "conscripted ... of the Irishry forever" by his great-grandmother having caught the famine-fever that a beggar from "the stricken west" passed on to her. Finding one's nation through infection, as posited by the poem, signifies the troubled, sick nature of colonisers and colonised sharing a troubled past which erodes as well as dismantles the initially imposed binary opposition between them. In the colonial narrative both parties tend to be "caught up in a complex reciprocity,"[3] characterising their increasingly entangled two-way relationship.

Recent research concerning the Famine as subject in Irish literature pinpoints the inherent difficulties of representation. According to Chris Morash,

> ... there is no single metanarrative of the Famine in literature. Instead, we
> find that the Famine as a textual event is composed of a group of images
> whose meaning does not derive from their strategic location within a narra-

---

[1] Luke Gibbons, "Ireland and the Colonization of Theory." *interventions* 1. 1 (1998), 27.

[2] Roy Foster, *Modern Ireland 1600-1972* (London: Penguin Books, 1989), 323-24.

[3] Ania Loomba, *Colonialism/Postcolonialism* (London: Routledge, 1998), 232.

tive, but rather from the strangeness and horror of the images themselves, as dislocated, isolated emblems of suffering.[4]

Not surprisingly, the literary inscriptions of the Famine taken together constitute a picture of ramifying polarities. Fictional works written close to the events themselves, like William Carleton's *The Black Prophet* (1847), emphasise the tragic conditions mainly in terms of the pervading horror. Several poems, composed in the mid- and later nineteenth century, were, in turn, tinged by an apocalyptic vision of colonialist history, advancing thus the nationalist cause.[5] Following them, the literary revivalists did not devote too much attention to the recent past, not even to the Famine, because to re-appropriate Irish difference they deemed it more suitable to reach back to legends rather than to history.[6] Set in Famine times, Yeats's *The Countess Cathleen* (1892) is no exception either, as it develops into a morality play about Anglo-Irish self-sacrifice for the Gaelic peasantry. The first novel to offer a detailed realistic portrayal of that painful segment of history, Liam O'Flaherty's *Famine* (1937) was written at a time when the young, independent Irish state was still in the process of defining itself.[7] A few years later, under the title *The Great Hunger* (1942), Patrick Kavanagh produced an anti-pastoral epic poem which highlighted the emotional and intellectual starvation of people living in tradition-bound rural Ireland, under the weight of inherited problems.

A significant bulk of Ireland's postcolonial literature has continued to engage with the identity-constructing narratives of the nation along with the internalisation of historical memories and the shadows and ghosts haunting those memories.[8] Inspired by the changing social and cultural climate of the 1960s, after the country had effectively started to emerge from her post-independence stagnation, the genre of drama managed to renew itself. Similarly to the avowed politics and aesthetics of the colonial renaissance of Irish drama, hallmarked by Yeats's, Synge's and Lady Gregory's contribution, the models and sources, again, had little connection with English theatre styles. Thomas Murphy's 1968 *Famine* reflects on the complex legacy of this significant seg-

---

[4] Christopher Morash, "Literature, Memory, Atrocities." Chris Morash and Richard Hayes (eds.), *Fearful Realities: New Perspectives on the Famine* (Dublin: Irish Academic Press, 1996), 114.

[5] Christopher Morash, *Writing the Irish Famine* (Oxford: Clarendon Press, 1995), 114-18.

[6] Seamus Deane, *Strange Country: Modernity and Nationhood in Irish Writing since 1790* (Oxford: Clarendon Press, 1997), 51.

[7] Margaret Kelleher, "The Irish Famine in Literature." Cathal Póirtéir (ed.), *The Great Irish Famine* (Dublin: Mercier, 1995), 241.

[8] Cf. Catherine Hall, "Histories, empires and the post-colonial moment." Iain Chambers and Lidia Curti (eds.), *The post-colonial question: common skies, divided horizons* (London: Routledge, 1996), 66.

ment of the colonial past deploying the form of the Brechtian epic drama, where the episodic structure promotes the creation of a shock "with which the single, well-defined situations of the play collide."[9] In the 1960s colonialist versions of Irish history were still alive, in fact enjoying a mini-renaissance under the banner of historical revisionism. Therefore, by its choice of theme and mode of presentation, Murphy's play embodies a kind of resistance, constructing a discursive counter-context in refutation of the orthodox and neo-orthodox readings of history.[10] Also, it re-confirms the connection between the damage of colonial conditions and some long-lasting, embarrassingly contradictory traits of the Irish national character itself.

Foregrounding the Perspective of the Colonial Other

The population of villages like the fictional Glanconor in the West of Ireland where the action of *Famine* takes place must have been still Gaelic-speaking during the years of the Great Famine. Murphy's play, however, is written in Hiberno-English, interspersed with structures re-sounding the native Gaelic while thoroughly hybridising the adopted medium, pointing thus to the two-way direction of language changes under colonisation. Through its indigenised version of English, *Famine* manages to emphasise the particular concerns of a non-English culture and give voice to one of its major narratives all the more forcefully for a postcolonial audience. At the same time, the text accommodates not a few expressions and short sentences in Gaelic, which convey shared communal values as well as individual feelings. Greetings, exclamations, curses, terms of intimacy and consolation make up this group, signifying that the deepest layers of subjectivity and the sense of belonging are likely to speak in the language that remained (relatively) intact from the colonial influence. Reinforcing the alterity, the distinct Irishness of the presented world, the performative aspects of the speech the people of Glanconor use in the play serve as important tools to "establish social registers that abrogate the privileged codes of the imperial standard."[11]

Restaging the past from the point of view of the colonial other, *Famine* exposes the traumatising experience of the Irish tenants whose life-sustaining crop has failed, jointly with the degrading and dehumanising nature of the imperialist practices. Through their fatal implications for the life of the characters in the given communal context, numerous crucial processes of the Famine

---

[9] Walter Benjamin, "What Is Epic Theatre?" *Illuminations*. Trans. Hannah Arendt. (New York: Schocken Books, 1978), 153.
[10] Cf. Helen Gilbert and Joanne Tompkins, *Post-colonial drama: theory, practice, politics* (London and New York: Routledge, 1996), 111-12.
[11] Ibid. 177.

and their corollary are re-presented by Murphy. The play begins focusing on loss: another daughter of the village leader, John Connor has perished from starvation and the wake is set in progress. The time is 1846, the Famine has already started and people anxiously discuss what they can expect. Murphy's work portrays it in its colonially determined reality, with references to previous, though lesser famines, thus putting the distortions of agriculture into a larger perspective. Out of the treasury of Irish traditions keening, the ritualised expression of grief over the death of family members and relatives appears both at the beginning and in the penultimate scene. Mother's words mourning her dead daughter find their echo in Dan's, the neighbour's incantatory keening for his wife:

> Cold and silent is now your bed, damp is the blessed dew of night but the sun will bring warmth and heat in the morning to dry up the dew. But your heart will feel no heat from the sun. No. Nor no more the track of your feet in the dew. No.... Cold and silent is now your bed. My sunshine you were, I loved you better nor the sun itself. And when I see the sun go down I think of my girl and the black night of sorrow. For a storm came on. And my girl cannot return.[12]

Thus, the Famine appears as a grief-ridden circle tightening around the people, followed by a new line mixing despair with some hope in the final scene when provisions have arrived and spring begins another cycle.

Scene Two sets the horrible contrast of the times into operation: while people are hopelessly digging for stray pieces of unblighted potato and whatever edible, nettle or roots, a convoy of corn-carts appears, on the way to export food products to England. Deprivation, to quote from an analysis, "coexisted with a thriving export trade and high profit margins, demonstrating the duality of the Irish economy."[13] "The Moral Force" as the title of Scene Two, rendered visible for the audience on a well-placed board in the theatre, works with the action ambiguously. The immorality of the colonial power taking all away from the starving native population pre-empts the possibility of moral behaviour: hunger and frustration generate violence. People, including the curate, turn against each other. John Connor accurately points to the humiliating change in people when he says: "They don't mean to be this way. It's only the hunger" (31). And anger does increase, in proportion with the expansion of disaster. In Scene Nine called "The Assassination," the organiser of the roadworks, the well-meaning though ineffectual Justice of the Peace is killed for not being able to employ everyone for the futile job. Ironically, the

---

[12] Thomas Murphy, *Famine* (Dublin: Gallery Books, 1977), 84. All further references are to this edition.
[13] Christine Kinealy, "Food Exports from Ireland 1846-47." *History Ireland* 5.1 (1997), 36.

distant colonial power remains inviolate, in spite of its evident responsibility. The evolution of individualism and selfishness form another side of what the demoralising circumstances bring about. More and more preoccupied with mere existence, people are shown hiding food and even stealing from each other, having lost their sense of community values as well as their sympathy for the plight of the fellow being.[14]

Scene Five, titled "The Relief Committee," is a remarkably detailed study of colonial attitudes among the village leaders. The Parish Priest argues in the interest of the famished people, representing the general benevolent commitment of the Catholic Church. The Justice of the Peace seeks to find a compromise between power and subjects, but in vain because he disregards apparent realities. Scarcely speaking during the scene, the Catholic merchant seems compliant with the system, motivated to place business interests higher than humanitarian considerations and altruistic feelings. Adopting the kind of discursive strategy that Homi K. Bhabha describes paradoxical because of connoting "rigidity and an unchanging order as well as disorder, degeneracy and daemonic repetition"[15] which fix the natives in racial and cultural difference, Captain, the Protestant landlord abuses them in the following terms:

> And did you ever try to get an honest day's work out of one of them? And their times of sowing: A month after the proper time. Not for want of encouragement.... Ignorance, deceit, rent evasion, begging. Filth, the breeding of disease ... But, are they so naturally this way—so naturally destructive? Hmm?... Coming in here this evening I passed some of their pig-sty dwellings and the chimneys are gone. (50-51)

Such deliberately malevolent stereotyping of the other provides the easiest excuse to evade responsibility for the situation. Murphy's Captain and Agent, who represents the absentee landlord, have drawn up a both cynical and self-serving plan for the solution of the problem. The starving villagers will be offered the financial means to emigrate, which is declared to be the only alternative to eviction and total dispossession. In the adjacent scene the interaction with the "clients" reconstructs the stigmatisation of the famine-stricken, sick-bodied people by "Make sure you do not breathe in this direction" (83) as a characteristic turn of speech on the part of the authority.

---

14 Thomas Gallagher, *Paddy's Lament: Ireland 1846-1847, Prelude to Hatred* (Swords: Poolbeg, 1988), 26-27.
15 Homi K Bhabha, *The Location of Culture* (London: Routledge, 1994) 66.

Images of Fragmentation and Paralysis

Imagining the Famine, as Chris Morash writes, projects images at the level of which "the body in pieces is inescapable."[16] Mourning a young girl's death in Scene One of *Famine* signifies the beginning of the fragmentation and dismembering of the village community's body. More fissures and ruptures appear in it when, oppressed by the situation, the people choose diverging paths of response like passive decline, violence, collaboration or emigration. The body being "the inscribed surface of events,"[17] Murphy's drama re-members the darkest time of colonial history by foregrounding disfigurement and decay. One of the younger villagers, Mickeleen O'Leary is a hunchback, the story of his life referring to parents who beat him into this state with a stick before they themselves starved to death on the hillside. His crippled figure establishes a link between the Famine and the violation of wholeness on the individual as well as on the community level, since his bitter spitefulness and mockery of virtually everything provoke quarrels and even violence. The tirade he launches at the wake in Scene One, "Did ye think '46 wouldn't folly *(follow)* '45? That bad doesn't folly bad? That all is to be bad! That ye'll all folly my style of thinking yet!" (22) sparks off the throwing of rotten potatoes at him and a ritual-like chase driving him away.

To paraphrase Frederic Jameson's idea with regard to strategies in Third-World texts, the story of individual destiny can be viewed as allegorical of the situation of a whole society.[18] Analogously, what happens to the main characters of *Famine* re-enacts the fundamental changes the Catholic Irish farmers suffered related to the Famine and colonial exploitation itself. As a site of both victimisation and scapegoating, Mickeleen's maimed body becomes a sign of the tragically paradoxical fortunes of a collective culture.[19] Mickeleen's brother, Malachy is back from England, having had experiences that enhanced his awareness of differences within the empire while he tried to earn money to help out his parents. On his home-coming, however, the distressing scene of "mother and father dead, the house tumbled and the holding gone" (39) welcome him. Radicalised by the overwhelming loss, Malachy advocates violence and then resorts to it by shooting the Justice of the Peace with a gun obtained from one of the policemen whose body he tossed in the quarry. The disguise he wears to avoid recognition when committing the deed functions also to be-

---

[16] Christopher Morash, "Famine/Holocaust: Fragmented Bodies." *Eire-Ireland* 1. 1 (1997), 147.

[17] Michel Foucault, "Nietzsche, Genealogy, History." Paul Rabinow (ed.), *The Foucault Reader* (London: Penguin Books, 1984), 83.

[18] Frederic Jameson, "Third-World Literature in the Era of Multinational Capitalism." *Social Text* 15 (1986), 69.

[19] Helen Gilbert and Joanne Tompkins, op. cit. 221.

speak the fatal transformations of the Irish colonial subject, involving both humiliation and violence. Malachy's face is blackened to resemble that of a Negro slave, parallelling the fact that the Irish were considered the Negroes of Europe, with "No Blacks, no Irish" as a frequently seen notice on houses that advertised rooms to let in England. Besides, there is a woman's dress over the young man's own clothes, reminiscent of the symbolic adoption of female gowns by rural insurgents in the eighteenth-nineteenth centuries, for instance the Molly Maguires in the west of Ireland.[20] Mickeleen and Malachy, both bearing Biblical names, often accompany or follow each other, their brotherly couple representing the two intertwined sides, imposed suffering and concomitant rebelliousness, of the historically shaped Irish character.

In *Famine*, the fate of those who have agreed to emigrate on board of the so called coffinships is suggested also in corporeal terms: they will arrive "on a foreign shore, the sacrifical offerings of a modern world" (58). Individual loss as well as the mutilation of the body of the community are brought into focus as famine-related experiential issues[21] by the increasing visibility of corpses in the drama. In Scene Four, "The Love Scene," the quasi-romantic orchestration of the meeting of Liam and Maeve in the moonlit forest is gravely undercut by the juxtaposition of dead and dying bodies. The sixteen-year-old girl behaves like *"a bitter old hag"* (43) in the early part of the scene, transforming back into her real being only when she has eaten of the apple that Liam dug up for her from a hole under the bushes. This change, however, is all too grotesque a counterpart of the one taking place at the closure of Yeats's *Cathleen ni Houlihan* (1902). It derives from sheer individualism feeding on embittered need, having virtually nothing to do with the pursuit of any common goal, as Liam has hidden away food for themselves while other villagers perish from starvation in their vicinity. "The Springtime" as title contextualises the concluding Scene Twelve, when food has come at last, but rebirth is made questionable by the enormity of human loss. John Connor calls the names of his family and the one-time community members, only to direct attention to their memory-haunting bodily absence or presence as putrid corpses. Self-degradingly, turning himself into a wreck as well in the moral sense, he has beaten his wife and son dead with a stick to save them from the horror of rotting away too slowly.

Bodily disintegration, understood both in individual and communial terms, is accompanied by mental/intellectual infection and disorder prevailing among

---

[20] Luke Gibbons, *Transformations in Irish Culture* (Notre Dame, Indiana: Univ. of Notre Dame Press, 1996), 141.
[21] Cf. Stanton B. Garner, Jr. *Bodied Spaces: Phenomenology and Performance in Contemporary Drama* (Ithaca: Cornell Univ. Press, 1994) 161.

the dispossessed. In Scene Eleven the feverish Dan rambles on about moments of Irish history as his memory retained them:

> Yis, sure I seen O'Connell once. Yis, yis, yis. The Liberator—didn't we, Brian? We did. And we waved. And he waved. And he smiled. On top of his horse. The lovely curly head on him. He did, did, waved with his hat.... Aaaa, but the day we got our freedom! Emancy-mancy—what's that, Nancy?—Freedom, boys! Twenty-nine was the year, and it didn't take us long putting up the new church. (86)

The activity of O'Connell, who initiated the decolonisation of Ireland by achieving Catholic emancipation in 1829, features here imbedded in a private story, indicating how little the oppressed people understood of the still so open-ended narrative of colonial history.[22] Emaciation overshadows the effects of emancipation in *Famine* and, the human context determined the way it is, "underneath the great official events of history, the wretched on the sidelines continue to be wretched."[23] Dan's raving story remains a jumble of fragments owing to the lived disharmony of individual experience and abstract political goals, disaster having desensitised people like him to the wider implications of noble though for the common mind all too distant ideas.

Connor, as Murphy characterises him in an article, is "a reluctant leader; leadership embarrasses him, impels him into outbursts of unreasonable resentment and into retreats of moody introspection."[24] His is the diametrical opposite of Malachy's approach who does not refrain from murder to arm himself and organises an attack on the authorities. Connor's position of village leader must account for this difference, at least to an extent. Trustful to the point of blindness and hesitant to act, he, at the same time, seems to embody the hybridised colonial subject, who accepts the unquestionable righteousness of the law and order maintained by the imperial power. In his view,

> It wasn't given to us to understand. A bitter man or a hungry man, or a dying man doesn't understand. But they're there, and for our good, and it's better we understand that. They have rules that they must follow, and we have one: to live and be as much at peace as we can with them, as with God. (*He pauses. Then, defiantly*) Well that's what I believe. I believe that. (40)

A train of thought like this testifies to Connor being thoroughly affected by "the non-exercise of private judgement and the exclusion of reasons in conflict

---

[22] Luke Gibbons, *Transformations in Irish Culture*, 158.

[23] Fintan O'Toole, *Tom Murphy: The Politics of Magic* (Dublin: New Ireland Books, 1994), 115-16.

[24] Thomas Murphy, "The Creative Process." Jacqueline Genet and Wynne Hillegouarc'h (eds.), *Irish Writers and the Creative Process* (Gerards Cross: Colin Smythe, 1996), 84.

with the authoritative reason."[25] His enunciation of dependence on the power "there" and his growing lack of control over the local situation are clear markers of the vast reduction of the agency of the native population, including its leaders. He is not maimed in body but paralysed in mind.

Traumatic Transformations

From the beginning of the drama Connor displays features like dutiful industry, patience and respect for as well as insistence on traditions. Feeling responsible for the community, he organises a meeting for the men in the village to discuss what steps should be taken, offering them hospitality in the spirit of the old ways despite the starvation of his own family. Fulfilling communal duties conscientiously, however, proves no longer compatible with what his private relations expect of him, which is getting enough food for them by whatever means. The roots of a long-standing, distressful (post)colonial personality trait can be detected here: the inability to bring one's respective loyalties to the public and private domains into harmony because the former demands too much of the individual. Besides, the gulf widens between these two due to the split the body of the community suffers as a result of the manifold, not only naturally but also historically determined disaster visiting a people already weakened by colonial mismanagement.

Hearts can turn to stone in such trying circumstances. Connor's lack of consideration for his family members derives from the destructiveness of the contradictory burden of the two-way responsibilities on him. Scene Eight configures the sinister signs of impending total disaster. At his wife's most practical advice, Connor has started to manufacture coffins for sale to obtain money or food. While working on one with a trap-bottom, he feels confused over the problem of whether the corpses will be carried on their faces in such a structure, which position evokes further humiliation of the already dead. Indifferent to the child's feelings, John uses his own son to investigate the best way the body can be placed in the coffin under construction, as if rehearsing for the inevitable, final performance that is closer and closer in view. On the other hand, Connor's wife, who has had to invent various survival strategies, including theft from fellow-sufferers, earns only resentment from her husband for her efforts. Despaired by their obvious difference regarding priorities that tears them apart and deepens the disintegration of the family, she feels herself "the slave of the slave," given "nothing but dependence" (85). An appropriate description, indeed, of the doubly oppressed and objectified position of the woman in the colonial society.

---

[25] Homi K Bhabha, op. cit. 112.

Often in literature "… images of 'the child' are deployed to stand in for humanitarian concern regarding crises of war and famine" and "'childhood,' like 'femininity,' stands in for and mediates larger social anxieties."[26] The disease or demise of a child recurs in several dramatic explorations of the most sensitive points of the Irish historical consciousness. In Stewart Parker's *Northern Star* (1984) the hero describes the failure of the United Irishmen's movement using the image of the child whose birth was botched. In Brian Friel's *Translations* (1980) and *Making History* (1988) the depth of the national tragedy is underscored by the report about a dead baby: the suppression of the Gaelic culture by nineteenth-century British colonisation in the one and the defeat of the Gaelic forces at the battle of Kinsale in the other. In *Making History* the mother is also lost, the entire crush of the revived Gaelic hopes being emphasised by the twin deaths, foregrounding individual tragedy to stage the private side of history versus the possible manipulations of the constructed public view. Even more complex is the national theme in Friel's *Faith Healer* (1979), with Frank at the end facing the group of wedding guests and the disabled McGarvey, whose innocent features and state of being protectively treated by his mates remind us also of a child, his infirmity bodying forth the inherited sickness of the community itself. Between the dead child and the crippled youth, on whom the two main stories of Friel's play hinge, Frank gives up, nevertheless having a "sense of home-coming."[27] In Murphy's later play *Bailegangaire* (1988), the prospective birth of a child brings relief and salvation as part of a new, promising national narrative set against the historical experience of grief and loss culminating in a child's death in fire.

The destructive effects of colonisation are present also in the breakdown of understanding between speakers of the same language, as individual words can develop vastly different meanings according to the users' links with or response to the system. In the vocabulary of *Famine* the word "right" gains a special position through being repeated by both the native and the colonialist characters in various interrelated contexts. The dramatist's strategy of juxtaposing and contrasting these linguistic aspects displays further divisions and the implications of the minds' disparate working in the colonial circumstances. In the usage of Connor the moral sense of "right" is paramount: people have to do what is right, that is wait for the government to take the necessary measures. It also refers to the justified expectations of the starving people as well as the moral duties of the authorities: "Help will come, because it's right. And what's right must be believed in if we're to hope" (40-41). However, his sense

---

[26] Jo-Ann Wallace, "Technologies of 'the child': towards a theory of the child subject." *Textual Practice* 9. 2 (1995), 287-88.
[27] Brian Friel, *Faith Healer. Selected Works* (Washington, D. C.: The Catholic Univ. of America Press, 1984), 376.

of "right" is fundamentally contradicted by the ideologised meaning of the same word when the Agent refers to it in his attempts to persuade Connor to choose emigration: "By signing the paper you will be doing the right thing" (66). At the end, in view of total deprivation Connor applies the word "right" without signification, as the world has lost its meaning for him. For Mother one implication of the word is still relevant: to have the right to die in as dignified a way as possible, which here is being beaten to death by her husband. The tragic absurdity underlying these linguistic changes is summed up by the Beckettian utterance of Dan, driven half-insane by suffering, beside the dead body of his wife: "Oh, I'm alright, and herself is worse" (82).

Conclusion

To complete the national allegory the play incorporates, calling the dead by name in the final scene like martyrs remoulding a device in folklore, John cannot but realise the size of loss surrounding him, along with the fact that all has changed—utterly. The other survivors, Maeve and Liam stand there like the Biblical couple driven out of the Paradise of living according to the old communal ways, the notion reinforced by their guilty eating of an apple beside the dying earlier in the play. Their repeated words, "we'll be equal to it" (87), signal determination to go ahead in spite of the waste and uncertainty they find themselves in. It is a closure performing an end that incarnates also a beginning, where the absence of the former world can be perceived "both as a utopian possibility for the future and as a reminder of human limitations inherited from the past."[28] Adding to the complexity of the scene, the professed courageousness of the young couple's attitude is contrasted by Maeve starting to cry when Liam, enacted as the final gesture in the play, places a piece of bread in her hand. These extremes in the behaviour of a survivor of the nation-wide trauma reflect the ambivalence informing the consciousness of the larger body of people, on the basis of the possible "analogy and symbiosis between the psychology of the nation and that of the individual."[29]

The play presents a fragment of the history of the Famine, with the action concluding in spring 1847 when "the historical worst was yet to come," in accordance with the author's conviction that full justice cannot be done to the actuality of those events.[30] But the open-endedness of the play also emphasises how unfinished the Irish past itself is, with "the seeds of violence, demoralisa-

---

[28] Christopher Morash, "Sinking Down Into the Dark: The Famine on Stage." *Bullán: An Irish Studies Journal* 3. 1 (1997), 85.

[29] Ciarán Benson, "A psychological perspective on art and Irish national identity." *The Irish Journal of Psychology* 15. 2, 3 (1994), 319.

[30] Thomas Murphy, "The Creative Process." 86.

tion and insecurity in modern Irish society"[31] having their origins in the Famine as a national disaster. Murphy's *Famine* re-imagines colonial times for the postcolonial present, fostering a better understanding and possible restructuring of identity features that keep confronting the Irish nation in the mirror of modern developments.

---

[31] Christopher Murray, *Twentieth-Century Irish Drama: Mirror up to Nation* (Manchester: Manchester Univ. Press, 1997), 183.

Cycling Pairs and Doubles in a House Divided Against Itself: Stewart Parker's *Spokesong*

Dramatising the Troubles

One of the central figures contributing to the contemporary renewal of Irish drama, Northern Irish playwright Stewart Parker (1941-1988) was born and educated in Belfast. As a young man, he had the opportunity to gain knowledge of the various manifestations of racism and the anti-racist struggle while teaching in the United States during the 1960s. His life took a dramatic turn when he resettled in his beloved hometown in 1969, virtually the same week that marked the beginning of the civil war called the Troubles. It was in the context of bombings and killings, but also when in spite of everything, many "succeeded in living normal lives, in rearing their children, doing a good job of work, being considerate neighbours, useful citizens,"[1] that he matured as playwright. Rejected in Belfast but becoming the hit of the Dublin Theatre Festival in 1975 his first stage success was *Spokesong*,[2] a play reflecting on sectarian violence in its own idiosyncratic way. Mahony contends that its merit lies in offering "a lighthearted approach to a serious subject that does not trivialise, but leaves the audience to search for answers to the many questions it raises."[3]

Among the plays addressing aspects of the political crisis and impasse in Northern Ireland, a considerable number employ a comparatively direct, documentary or even naturalistic approach, including Sam Thompson's *Over the Bridge* (1960), John Boyd's *The Flats* (1971), Bill Morrison's *Flying Blind* (1977), Graham Reid's *The Closed Door* (1980), and Martin Lynch's *The Interrogation of Ambrose Fogarty* (1982), to name but a few. Others choose non-realistic, frequently metaphorical or allegorical modes of referring to the Troubles and its bearing on individual lives. Parker's *Spokesong* has affinities and shares certain features with this second group, where one can find Brian Friel's *The Freedom of the City* (1973) and *Volunteers* (1975), David Rudkin's *Ashes* (1974) and *The Saxon Shore* (1986), Anne Devlin's *Ourselves Alone* (1985), Frank McGuinness's *Carthaginians* (1988) and so forth. To analyse the political relevance of these plays necessitates a redefinition of what the

---

[1] Ciaran Brady, Mary O'Dowd, Brian Walker (eds.), *Ulster, An Illustrated History* (London: B. T. Batsford Ltd., 1989), 218.
[2] Christopher Murray, *Twentieth-century Irish Drama: Mirror up to Nation* (Manchester: Manchester Univ. Press, 1997), 196.
[3] Christina Hunt Mahony, *Contemporary Irish Literature: Transfroming Tradition* (London: Macmillan, 1998), 172.

term 'political' implies with regard to the contemporary theatre. *The Politics of Theatre and Drama* by Graham Holderness, which scrutinises the subject from an international perspective, arrives at the conclusion that;

> ... the political character of a cultural form should be sought only in the politics of form—estranging, alienating, self-reflexive—and its politics of function—de-stabilising the conventional relation between spectator and performance, disrupting traditional expectations of narrative and aesthetic coherence, de-familiarising and interrogating the oppressive power of naturalised cultural forms.[4]

In this sense, Parker's experimental play can be viewed as political inasmuch as it dramatises life in the 1970s by patterning a series of dualities pervading form, structure as well as character, to illuminate the fundamentally split nature of both the history and the society of Belfast.

As the author himself claims, *Spokesong* "tries to isolate what is at the heart of the turbulence in Ireland at the moment. But I decided against writing a play about Protestants and Catholics ... That would only be dealing with the surface, anyway. I wanted to go underneath all that and look at the core."[5] Elsewhere, in his account of the play's genesis, he maintains when writing *Spokesong* that he aimed "to construct a working model of whole-ness by means of which this society can begin to hold up its head in the world."[6] Set alternatingly in the present and the past, the action takes place in and out of a bicycle shop situated in "a house divided against itself,"[7] which is in Belfast, the city divided according to the sectarian schism in the historically partitioned Ireland. Wholeness appears to be achievable only by moving beyond the immediate, the whole having to grow out of the 'hell-hole' of brutal mundane reality. The play itself grasps and presents a complexity of facts and feelings which run parallel or counter to each other, maintaining creative tension and dramatic suspense at the same time.

---

[4] Graham Holderness, "Introduction." Graham Holderness, (ed.), *The Politics of Theatre and Drama* (London: Macmillan, 1992), 13.

[5] Qtd. in Robert Berkvist, "A Freewheeling Play About Irish History." *The New York Times*, 11 March 1979, 4.

[6] Qtd. in Claudia W. Harris, "The Flame That Bloomed." *The Irish Literary Supplement*, Spring 1989, 4.

[7] Stewart Parker, *Spokesong* (New York: Samuel French, Inc., 1980), 61. All further references are to this edition.

Doubling Scenes and Themes

Action is essentially discontinuous in *Spokesong*.[8] Its two-act composition can be described as resting on a design of doubling: scenes refer to each other, strengthen or undercut meanings by their juxtaposition, pairing or contrast. At the beginning, a figure named in the cast the Trick Cyclist appears in a variety-act uniform riding a unicycle and singing the happy 'Daisy Bell' song, after which he transforms himself into a public servant interviewing a man called Frank Stock. In the ensuing dialogue Frank, the protagonist, who is initially a spokesman because he repairs bicycles, turns out to embody an inspired advocate of and spokesman for the rediscovery of the "faithful bicycle" (11), over and against plans for building one more motorway for vehicles with internal combustion engines. The unreality of the scene suggests its taking place in mental and emotional terrains, in the form of a constant interior debate with the hostile powers of the world. This metaphorical action is followed by an earthly one: the first meeting of Frank and schoolteacher Daisy in the former's bicycle shop. The juxtaposition of the two scenes introduces two planes, one in the mind where desires are conceived and travels elsewhere are possible without limit, and the other in everyday reality.

Calling into being alternative worlds, the "central, dramatic tension" in Parker's play is "between what a man feels life ought to be and the thwarting, hostile reality of what is."[9] The parallels and contrasts of the ideal and the real are elaborated and enriched in scope by patterning shifts between the present and the past, imaginary and real scenes, songs and dialogues, building up a fragmented structure. The actions and conversations recalled from Frank's grandparents' life complement what is going on in the present, in fact they seem to be evoked by it. The past is experienced subjectively, internalised, as Frank confesses: "It's not a question of remembering. They are me. A big part of me" (60). Thus the duet between him and history-teaching Daisy recalls the scene of bicycle-fanatic Francis wooing a hard-headed girl named Kitty who wished that Ireland and womanhood gain sovereignty simultaneously. Continuity within the family is reinforced by the virtually identical first names of the men, as well as by their surname being Stock, a reminder of where Frank comes from.[10] In a Wildean fashion, Frank gives his name as "Francis John Boyd Dunlop Stock" (10), to indicate his roots precisely. With regard to the female protagonists, the red-haired, bicycle-liberated Kitty, a kind of New Woman is the namesake of her historical contemporary, Katharine O'Shea,

---

[8] Elmer Andrews, "The Power of Play: Stewart Parker." *Theatre Ireland* 18, April-June 1989, 24.
[9] Ibid. 24.
[10] Christopher Murray, op. cit. 197.

Parnell's independent-minded and morally courageous mistress, then devoted wife. Daisy, on the other hand, wears a rather common name borrowed from the extensively quoted folksong 'Daisy Bell.' Unlike her namesake in F. Scott Fitzgerald's *The Great Gatsby* who turns away from the dreamer, she decides to remain with the idealist Frank.

On the public level, however, a gap opens between past and present. In the past the universal acceptance of the common wheel was also questioned, but for different reasons: rigorous Victorian morality had its objections to it. Nevertheless, it eventually contributed to women's long overdue emancipation. In the Great War the bicycle was used for military purposes, so Francis's idealism was also subject to the blows of reality and history. Differently though again, the story of the Army Cyclist Corps, for whom "it is imperative that the cyclist should not allow his machine to fall intact into the enemy's hands" (49), is told with so much amusement. In the present, Frank's dream-world of all mankind peacefully riding bikes is contrasted with the traps of 1970s reality, which gradually envelope his Victorian shop in the course of the play. Firstly the audience hears about the City Redevelopment Plans menacing small properties like his; then, with the reappearance of his foster brother Julian it becomes obvious that the cruel fraternal hostilities of Northern Ireland confront Frank's and others' path to individual, bicycle-symbolised freedom. In addition, the explosion of bombs and the death of innocent citizens, such as the nearby petshop owner, loom large in the background. Daisy claims that the teenagers at her school have experienced history by the time they enter the classroom, "fresh in from stoning soldiers, and setting fire to shops" (35), ironically counterpointing Frank's idealism.

Themes continue to appear in two lights, the validity of the private perspective, however, being significantly overshadowed by the public narrative that dominates day-to-day life in the province. At the end of Act One, Daisy and Frank disagree about the meaning of history. His way of looking at it is genuinely subjective: "I don't see the truth in battles or the lives of the celebrated megalomaniacs. That's not the important history either. I see it in all the things that ordinary people do with their time" (35). This argument is strongly called into question by the intrusion of Daisy's reference to a hard-boiled fact of contemporary reality: "My father's one of the neighbourhood gangsters" (36). The juxtaposed scene recalled from the past leads the Trick Cyclist on stage clothed in an Irish Guards major's uniform of the Boer War. He is the father of Kitty, hostile to the union of his daughter and Francis. Once again, the bicycle image and the freedom associated with it becomes challenged by authority figures, in this case represented by the two fathers who subscribe to the use of guns in the process of shaping history.

At the beginning of Act Two wars in the past and in the present are set against each other, along with people's varying attitudes to them. Francis's dislike of violence and instinctive search for self-defence while serving in the World War One Army Cyclist Corps is flanked by a scene following the explosion of a bomb in the present. The Trick Cyclist, this time as leather-jacketed Duncan, Daisy's father, capitalises on the fact that ordinary people can be frightened into paying for the privilege of having their premises left intact. Violence and war reappear in the mention of a bomb which killed Frank's parents. In Kitty's words: "They were killed by a German bomb. If Ireland had been a united country it wouldn't have been dropped" (54). The latter part of her statement rings true also of the preceding scene, with its violence and murderous explosion in the present. Nevertheless, a parallel idea blunts the appeal of Kitty's nationalist explanation: it was a cat's eczema, according to old Francis, that helped to change the family's history because it helped him meet John Dunlop. This return to the importance of the bicycle disguises Frank's desperate reaching out for comfort in the family past and its inheritance, because of his first-hand experiences of terrorism topped by Julian's having sold his shop to be turned into a terrorist headquarters. The imagined family scene helps him to momentarily accept his present in terms of the past: "Love, war and the bicycle ... the gist of their lives ... mine too. My love, my war, my bicycle" (56). But violence returns in the next scene where Daisy's story about the schoolchildren's terrorist deeds is presented to justify her decision to clear out for good and leave Frank homeless and dispossessed in more than one sense. Finally, after darkness has almost won, a miraculous ending lifts Frank, and also the play, out of their staggering deadlock: circumstances awakened Daisy to see through Julian and come back to Frank.

The scenes from the years gone by, fictionalised and restaged in Frank's mental theatre, enact his obsession with the past and its old-fashioned values. He is reliving and reinterpreting the past of his own bicycle-loving family, which provides him with moral strength and rectitude despite his daily experiences of an unstable present and an evidently unforseeable future. Thus the ideal in the play can barely be separated from the nostalgia for past values. Frank's nostalgia, however, is not entirely blind: after the first evoked scene between Francis and Kitty there follows a direct switch to Frank who muses on their doings. In the second part of the drama, distressed and dismayed amidst the encircling mud of sectarian violence, he speaks directly to Francis and claims that "It is not just the same as it was for you. There's no simple enemy. There's no Back Home. No Boche. And no Blighty" (64-65). The grandparents fade out of the picture when the impending but ultimately unrealised betrayal of Daisy has further disappointed Frank, who finds his new solace in the bottle and the company of the Trick Cyclist. He is at his lowest, acknowledging personal defeat: "Say what you like ... the bicycle has a great past ahead of it ... I came to be a pacifist, a philosopher and a lone wolf by the age of seven." A pair of slang words serve to sum up his sense of helplessness: he describes himself as a static and ineffectual "bouncer" opposed to the vigorous mobility of "breakers" (70-71).

Splitting Identity

The two half-brothers, Frank and Julian are both complementary and contradictory, conceived in harmony with the tendency in the Irish theatre that Anthony Roche describes in terms of moving away "from the idea of a single leading man and towards the sharing of the stage space between two male protagonists."[11] Beginning in the plays of W. B. Yeats and Samuel Beckett, then characterising the art of Brian Friel, Thomas Kilroy, Thomas Murphy and others, several such pairs occur with the role of articulating both individual and communal attitudes, relationships and psychological concerns. The tension between Parker's two males avoids repeating the pattern of the sectarian divide which would easily lend itself to scrutiny considering the locus of action in the drama. Their division has a recognisably moral basis, to demonstrate that polarised varieties of identity and self-definition do not necessarily depend upon internalised religious and ethnic difference.

Frank represents the idealist advocating naively good common wheel plans and general humanitarianism, whose "bicycle-philosophy" rests on the assumption that "So far as personal transport goes—the bicycle was the last advance in technology that everybody understands" (19). For him, it is the embodiment of a whole set of values like harmony, peace, and fraternity; because "bicycles are human" (13). What is more, even Christ can be thought of as riding a bicycle. Frank declares the bicycle's superiority to the automobile, in which bombs can be planted, and also to the aeroplane, which makes the passenger feel helpless and estranged. Yet his idealism blends with distancing self-irony; a case in point being when he gives his theatricised account of the inquiry following his proposal to the authorities: "Enter a happy idiot advocating the bicycle solution. Nobody smiles. ... They stare at me in fear" (33).

With his doggedly optimistic eulogies about an old-fashioned vehicle, his long-lasting trust and ever-renewed daydreaming, followed by a spectacular collapse, Frank is also seen as considerably comic. To highlight this ambivalence, the play, abounding in literary allusions and intertextuality, quotes the romantic poet Wordsworth in two different ways. When rehearsing for the public inquiry, nature-loving Frank uses the line "Earth would not have anything to show more fair" (28) from *Composed Upon Westminster Bridge, September 3, 1802* as an argument for a world of bikes with clean air and energy conservation. The early morning beauty of the city in the poem is, how-

---

11 Anthony Roche, *Contemporary Irish Drama: From Beckett to McGuinness* (Dublin: Gill and Macmillan, 1994), 79.

ever, felt to be transient, because daytime activities have not begun yet to pollute the "smokeless air." Once Frank's early enthusiasm is deflated by the accumulation of negative experiences, and he has taken to drinking in the company of the Trick Cyclist, he distorts a Wordsworthian title (*Ode; Intimations of Immortality from Recollections of Early Childhood*) along with starting to destroy himself, saying: "… let me tell you about this beautiful old shop … herewith, An Ode! Intimations of Negativity in Late Childhood" (71).

Julian's character is directly opposed to that of Frank, he incarnates cynicism, lack of consideration and hatefulness, which he calls a sense of reality. On the other hand, he is introduced as being seen by two different people. For Frank he is a troublemaker who undermines the remaining peace of the present, while for Daisy he acts as a newcomer bringing excitement. The contrast between the two brothers is enhanced by Parker's choice of names: Frank (like his grandfather, Francis) recalls the legendary Francis of Assisi, a saint of peace and kindness particularly devoted to nature and humanistic deeds. The half-brother figure bears the name of Julian the Apostate, the Roman emperor whose "policy was to degrade Christianity and promote paganism by every means short of open persecution."[12] In a powerful dialogue between the two, Julian tries to ridicule Frank's humanistic feelings but turns out repeating slogans of destructiveness, even terrorism. It is the idealist Frank who points to a workable use of the past for the sake of life in the present:

> JULIAN   Look at yourself. Hunkered down in this … blocked-up latrine of
> your own memories. That's what memories are, big brother,
> that's what the past is, history, the accumulated turds of human
> endeavour. I don't like it, I'm a cleanly fellow. It has to come
> down, the whole edifice, brick by brick. Wiped. flushed.
>
> FRANK   Have you not learned anything at all? You *are* your own past,
> kid. You're the sum total of its parts. Hate it and you hate
> yourself. No matter how calamitous it may have been, either you
> master it or die. (60-61)

However, Julian's 'reality' proves to be nothing but corruption, he is unmasked as a turncoat. Daisy chooses to live with Frank, and the lovers mount their tandem in faith and merrily wheel out of the play, but not without the awareness that their happiness is privately owned, while the city is still the same. Daisy's remark to the effect that changes have to be made may as well bear reference not only to the shop and its business but to the larger scene. The audience, on the other hand, might easily be reminded of the fate of Nagg and Nell in *Endgame* by Parker's greatest influence, Beckett, who lost their

---

[12] F. L. Cross, E. A. Livingstone (eds.), *The Oxford Dictionary of the Christian Church* (Oxford: Oxford Univ. Press, 1988), 765.

shanks while on a ride on their tandem and became reduced to ashcan-en-tombed human wrecks.

On a more concrete level, Frank's and Daisy's brittle happiness is undercut by Julian's callous robbing of the till aided by the Trick Cyclist. The latter's merry song courts Daisy Bell, as at the beginning, but its sweetness is not able to dispel the poison of mixed feelings in the air. According to Parker, the play "ends on an ambiguous note, but not a pessimistic one."[13] Even strong believers like Frank, whose bicycle-religion suggests the transcendability of sectarian opposition, have access only to hardearned private solutions while public reality remains an unconquerable stone "in the midst of all." The common wheel of a bicycle cannot guarantee a different ending for a divided common-weal, as it would demand more energy and co-operation than two people can provide. With "two brothers fight[ing] over the inheritance of a bicycle shop"[14] where one owns the house and the other runs the business, Parker creates a metaphorical reference to the identity divisions in Northern Ireland carrying the threat of hostility and violence. Julian is not merely a Cain-like figure but a warning that out of the union of Catholic and Protestant—as his parents are described—a very dubious mixture may result. Called to mind by the motif of split central to the brothers' relationship and used in the title of the present paper, the continuation of Jesus's words in *The New Testament* suggests a dubious future for the province of Northern Ireland as well: "Every kingdom divided against itself is laid waste, and no city or house divided against itself will stand" (Matthew 12. 22).

Metatheatre and Metaphor

Spokesong strikes its audience as highly and captivatingly theatrical, a feature bound up with its holding more than one plane of reality "in ambiguous suspension" whereas purporting "to express the relative and multiple nature of self-identity."[15] The Trick Cyclist's opening song is followed by sentences which sound like an address to two audiences: one at the meeting dealing with Frank's plans and the other in the theatre: "I'll just say a word or two to those of you who have come here for the first time. We're all present for the purpose of an inquiry into matters of great importance affecting every one of us" (9). Borrowing the words of the play's author again, *Spokesong* well deserves to be described as a product of "an unconscious impulse to express the most

---

[13] Qtd. in Robert Berkvist, op. cit. 8.

[14] Philomena Muinzer, "Evacuating the Museum: the Crisis of Playwriting in Ulster." *New Theatre Quarterly* 3. 9 (1987), 49.

[15] Elinor Fuchs, *The Death of Character: Perspectives on Theatre after Modernism* (Bloomington and Indianapolis: Indiana Univ. Press, 1996), 33.

ancient element in playacting—the instinct for play itself."[16] Its very title is a funny-sounding compound of a pair of one-syllable words suggesting the fusion of prosaic reality and transcending music, reinforced by the fact that "spoke" has two distinct meanings. The use of puns and rich verbal ironies remains characteristic throughout.

Anticipating the strategy deployed in *Northern Star* (1984), Parker reinscribes elements of the style of earlier playwrights to underscore the interaction with the past on the artistic level. In a scene enacting the late nineteenth century family history two contemporary writers are mentioned side by side, known and remembered by the couple for divergent reasons. Arthur Conan Doyle is relevant as the author of a short story entitled *The Solitary Cyclist,* in which the detective Sherlock Holmes, defender of law and order, explores a case involving the use of bicycles. The other literary giant, Oscar Wilde, represents art and eccentric freedom, and the spirit of his drama is recaptured in Parker by the Wildean wit spicing the language of Kitty, Daisy and Julian,[17] for instance in the following dialogue:

FRANCIS	... Kitty—can I—may I—return to the subject of my proposal.
KITTY	Which proposal? Oh yes—you were proposing to call upon my father. You may certainly visit my father any time you like, Francis.
FRANCIS	My dearest!
KITTY	Personally I shall find nothing that he might say of any interest. It certainly won't have the slightest influence over me.
FRANCIS	You mean ... you won't marry me?
KITTY	You haven't yet asked me. (23)

The omnipresence of the bicycle and especially its final metamorphosis into a tandem, "a new model" (73), lends the play an atmosphere of wishing for harmony and peace. After all, the two wheels of a bicycle can do their job only in unison if any kind of progress is intended. This all-pervading metaphor becomes a powerful reminder of basic human needs. Deployed both physically and metaphorically, it is the bicycle that establishes a connection between the ideal and the real. As part of the folklore of Belfast, where John Dunlop invented the pneumatic tyre in 1887, the bicycle is related to both the city and its people. Unionist and Nationalist, as Francis and Kitty remain, they are united by the bike. As opposed to the discontinuous history of the six counties it has, according to Frank's triumphant assessment of it, one which displays an ongoing fulfilment of human visions ever since wheeled vehicles

---

[16] Stewart Parker, "State of Play." *The Canadian Journal of Irish Studies* 7. 1 (1981), 9.

[17] Michael Etherton, *Contemporary Irish Dramatists* (New York: St. Martin's Press, 1989), 23.

started to be used in Lower Mesopotamia in 3,500 B. C. Thus he reinforces the transcending nature and liberating role of harmonious ideals which help people find the centre of their lives and keep above the tide of distress. At the same time, the continuity of human life is emphasised in spite of all drastic historical changes.

A different vehicle is ridden by the Trick Cyclist, the entertainer/trickster who plays a good number of minor characters, real as well as imaginary across the past, present and mythic time, establishing contact between ordinary action and the spiritual realm of reflecting on it.[18] In one figure he unites both good and devilish features, his music-hall-like performance of singing and dancing contrasted by his transformation into gangster, political hoodlum and army officer in a long and disastrous war, suggesting the puzzling variety of manifestations of human potential. Both his name and his vehicle are related to tricks and deception, the opposite of honesty and frankness. In the last scenes, however, as Frank's companion in self-destruction and of Julian's in plundering the till, he appears to enact the respective shadows of both, bypassing any rigid dualism. The disillusioned and desperate Frank describes his loss of faith with the words: "God's a bad trick cycling act" (72).

Is the Trick Cyclist a reminder of the lurking evil in man whose bicycle-happy songs fill the air only to generate false beliefs? There is no clear answer. A figure from the Irish folk tradition and "basically destructive and mischievous,"[19] his in-and-out presence in the play parallels and also contrasts that of the bicycle, since he is more than one of the characters, like the bicycle which serves as more than a well-known means of transport in the play. Through his contradictory roles and endless performing, he becomes a metaphor for the liminality of the Northern Irish context, defying the belief in easy solutions despite private desires and idealism. Evil may emerge where it is least expected. The Trick Cyclist embodies features which are latent in people, therefore he criss-crosses the stage in different guises and under different masks, appealing and repelling in turn. But his unicycle is by no means a common weal, perhaps thus also referring to man's essential loneliness and, lamentably, selfishness.

Spokesong is a serio-comic play in which a lot of singing is used to assert individual as well as communal feelings, similar to other 'Troubles-plays' like Patrick Galvin's *We Do It for Love* (1975), where the central metaphor is a Merry-Go-Round. Blending prose drama with the features of the musical, the richness of Parker's effects includes charm and vivid humour, mostly produced by the wit and colloquialisms of its language. At the same time there is

---

[18] Cf. Helen Gilbert and Joanne Tompkins, *Post-colonial drama: theory, practice, politics* (London and New York: Routledge, 1996), 142.
[19] Alan Harrison, *The Irish Trickster* (Sheffield: Sheffield Academic Press, 1989), 24.

some vague sense of fear that all the mirth may prove so brittle. Artistic and at times falling to pieces, *Spokesong* puzzles the audience by its theatrical double-dealing. It shows the wholeness of existence both funny and disturbing, promising and distressing in which hardly anything has a uniform face. Reflecting on the Troubles from a unique point of view, *Spokesong* delicately balances two planes: one is the level of desire for harmony, love and peace, while the other is that of inconsideration, thirst for vengeance, and hatred. That the two have possible meeting points and sometimes even overlap, is tellingly underscored by Daisy finally dismissing Julian with the words: "You are a worse clown than your brother. You're pathetic" (69).

The city development plans, while endangering the future use of the bicycle as they do, mean the reconstruction of bomb damaged buildings. Through its absurdities this funny play emphasises the abnormality of the situation in Northern Ireland, but does not leave the audience with the feeling that violence and destruction rule uncontested. Through thick and thin, the object and metaphor of the bicycle, with its harmoniously running wheels provides a frame to the fluid matter which is equally fragile and strong. The protagonist's, Frank's job also functions on the metaphorical level, as he is engaged in putting pieces together, repairing what does not operate adequately. In this respect it seems justifiable to compare him with Wilson John Haire's The Buck Lep, a figure with a tremendous resource of humour and helpfulness occupied as a (rebuilding) mason in the author's 'Troubles play,' *Bloom of the Diamond Stone* (1973).

Spokesong in the Parker Canon

Parker's greatest plays focusing on his homeland follow *Spokesong* by several years, when he had more awareness of what the "great flat thick slab of granite" infused with "a rich vein of humanity" (58) in Daisy's description about the province was. Developing the technique of doubles and parallels further, both *Northern Star* and *Pentecost* (1987) connect the discourses of present and past as inseparable in Northern Ireland, underpinned by the presence of ghosts on the stage in the manner of *Spokesong*.[20] At the same time, in their own ways, they temper the deterministic view of history and politics by images of hope and freedom. *Northern Star* contrasts the decline and ultimate failure of the United Irishmen's movement and rebellion by the flourishing development of the Irish theatre from the language of which Parker borrows to mediate history. Its protagonist, Henry McCracken echoes much of Frank's idealism as well as ironical self-theatricalising, based on a historical figure whose appeal for Parker lay in his being "a practical joker and gifted mimic ... apparently

---

[20] Cf. Christina Hunt Mahony, op. cit. 171.

without sectarian prejudice."[21] McCracken considers Northern Ireland as a locus of identity divisions, "with two men fighting over it. Cain and Abel."[22] Yet his ambition to make peace between antagonistic factions fails, and it is only in *Pentecost,* a play "about healing rifts"[23] in the present, that human reconciliation finally takes place under a clear sky in Belfast.

Due to the author's "basic dynamic outlook"[24] and treasury of theatrical devices (re)cycling pairs, doubles and fusing polarised modes of expression, in *Spokesong* values like love, honesty and care for other people illuminate even the darkest moments. The surrounding hostile reality never appears strong enough to obliterate dreams of wholeness, humanism and the wish to play. Constructed under the impact of the most threatening phase of the Troubles, *Spokesong* joins itself to the Irish dramatic tradition by its attempt to heal and transcend while effectively manipulating an ever so rich arsenal of art.

---

[21] Marilynn Richtarik, "Living in Interesting Times: Stewart Paker's *Northern Star.*" John P. Harrington and Elizabeth J. Mitchell (eds.), *Politics and Performance in Contemporary Northern Ireland* (Amherst: Univ. of Massachusetts Press, 1999), 12.

[22] Stewart Parker, *Northern Star. Three Plays for Ireland* (Birmingham: Oberon Books, 1989), 57.

[23] Claudia W. Harris, "From Pastness to Wholeness: Stewart Parker's Reinventing Theatre." *Colby Quarterly* 27. 4 (1991), 240.

[24] Elmer Andrews, "The Will to Freedom: Politics and Play in the Theatre of Stewart Parker." Okifumi Komesu and Masaru Sekine (eds.), *Irish Writers and Politics* (Gerrards Cross: Colin Smythe, 1989), 268.

"Ireland mustn't be such a bad place, so, if the Yanks want to come here to do their filming." Reflections on the West and Irishness in Martin McDonagh's Plays

Introduction

Rarely does it happen nowadays that a still under-thirty playwright makes a remarkably successful debut in the world of the theatre with as many as four plays and wins a couple of awards for them in the span of only two years. The recently emerged Martin McDonagh is such an author, moreover, a kind of *enfant terrible* whose so far completed works offer a shockingly ruthless and unsentimental picture of the West of Ireland. His background includes parents from Connemara and Sligo respectively, but he himself lives in London and has developed a keen interest in roots.[1] It is during his frequent visits to Galway that he picks up ideas for his works.[2] Writing about the West of Ireland, McDonagh finds it a more than obvious necessity to confront the question of how place shapes and determines identity. From among those playwrights who have been in this terrain before, the dramatic heritage of Synge seems to incarnate the greatest challenge for him and he boldly enters the palimpsest, a process so overwhelmingly characteristic of contemporary Irish playwriting.[3] His re-inscription of Synge consists of assimilating, restructuring, deconstructing as well as parodying themes and motifs from *The Playboy of the Western World*.

McDonagh's special strength, however, lies not only in re-engaging the colonial theme and inverting it, but also in his mapping of postmodern complexities. He is well aware of the fact that the sense of space has altered by our time, the intrusion of the media having enlarged the world for the individual, expanding it from the local towards the global. The West of Ireland being a geographical and historical unit as well as a cultural construct, McDonagh's strategy is to dramatize a view of the changing communal and individual values of the territory interspersed with renegotiated myths and images deriving from other discourses, texts and art forms. Thematizing the "ambiguous relations between image and reality, problematized by the manipulation of the au-

---

1 Joseph Feeney, SJ, "Martin McDonagh: Dramatist of the West." *Studies: An Irish Quarterly Review*, Spring 1998, 26.
2 Rupert Christiansen, "Eight days that changed a couch potato's life." *The Sunday Telegraph*, March 17, 1996. 9.
3 Cf. Christopher Murray, "The State of Play: Irish Theatre in the 'Nineties." Eberhard Bort (ed.), *The State of Play: Irish Theatre in the 'Nineties* (Tübingen: Wissenschaftlicher Verlag Trier, 1996), 20.

dience's response,"[4] his theatre reifies an essential aspect of the postmodern experience. On the other hand, as a postcolonial author he turns critically to the new imperialism of certain media systems "that reinforce hierarchies based on race, gender, ethnicity, religion, sexual preference, and class."[5] McDonagh's interrogation of life in the West of Ireland along with the set of cultural codes surrounding as well as invading it finds its natural parallel in Sam Shepard's revisioning the myths about the West in American culture, most notably in his *True West* (1980). Shepard qualifies as a precursor also because his postmodern dramatic language uses images "from the mythological to the medialogical"[6] in a stunning variety of ways. The purpose of the present paper is to discuss how and with what effect intertextual motifs and media-references contribute to McDonagh's unique reflection on the dialectics between place and identity in his so far completed four plays about the West of Ireland.

The Beauty Queen of Leenane

The Beauty Queen of Leenane (1996), although set in "recognisable, rooted reality," exposes "a terrible rootlessness" lying at the centre of its portrayed community according to the view of theatre director Garry Hynes.[7] The main characters, a mother (Mag) and a daughter (Maureen) live in a rural cottage in Connemara. Their relationship resembles the one between Christy Mahon and his father: the selfish parent dominates the child who tries to strike back. The masculine context of the limiting pressure of the old order under the colonial circumstances has been replaced by the feminine, as in postcolonial Ireland the theme of identity often centers around the woman, "marginalised ... devalued and minimalised" by patriarchal power and the remnants of the imperialist culture.[8] Like a vicious parody of the Mother-Ireland figure who exploits her child demanding its self-sacrifice, Mag incarnates past-ridden restrictions that block the way of Maureen's growing up and escape from the delimiting circumstances. Recalling Synge's protagonist, the daughter cherishes dreams "Of

---

[4] Maria Tymoczko, "A Theatre of Complicity." Review of Martin McDonagh's *The Beauty Queen of Leenane. Irish Literary Supplement*, Fall 1997. 16.
[5] Helen Gilbert and Joanne Tompkins, *Post-colonial drama: theory, practice, politics* (London: Routledge, 1996), 277.
[6] Cf. Una Chaudhuri, *Staging Place: The Geography of Modern Drama* (Ann Arbor: The Univ. of Michigan Press, 1997), 113.
[7] Qtd. in Clare Bayley, "A new voice for Ireland." *Independent*, 28 Febr., 1996. 7.
[8] Wanda Balzano, "Irishness—Feminist and Post-colonial." Iain Chambers and Lidia Curti (eds.), *The post-colonial question: common skies, divided horizons* (London: Routledge, 1996), 93.

anything! ... Of anything. Other than this."[9] Mag's tyrannical bossiness and infantile self-centeredness provoke her into violent reaction: she tortures her mother by spilling hot oil on the latter's hand. She even wishes her mother dead in order to emancipate herself and put an end to "being stuck up here" (15), envisaging an attack on her mother "with a big axe or something" (6) to take her head off and split her neck, echoing Christy Mahon's stories of his imagined patricide. The destructive mother-daughter relationship evoked by McDonagh is surrounded by the mean conflicts and hatreds of the tight, claustrophobic world of Leenane, abundant in brutality but lacking spiritual centre or guidance. The priest of the community remains an off-stage figure, but while in *The Playboy* the similarly positioned Father Reilly embodies an authority still held in some respect, McDonagh's Father Welsh has become a mere object of ridicule with his family name repeatedly mistaken for Walsh.

To escape their boredom, unease of belonging and communicational impasse the inhabitants of McDonagh's small town frequently escape to the dubious messages of the media. Certain programmes gain strategic significance in *The Beauty Queen* by underscoring the disunity of subjective experience in the electronic society that is without the safety of a fixed point of departure in both time and space for the orientation of the individual.[10] The broadcasting in Gaelic by Radio Eireann attempts to serve the estimated needs of the people to reunite themselves with the cultural traditions of their area. However, the native language made available to them through such regular programmes falls on deaf ears in the case of the old hag, Mag. She considers it meaningless babble not worth listening to: "Why can't they just speak English like everybody?" (4). Maureen's reaction is to resort to clichés and stereotypical remarks concerning the historical loss of the Gaelic language and the grievances of the Irish people. Also on the radio, the singing of *The Spinning Wheel* by Delia Murphy, revived from the 1950-60s, intends to rekindle people's admiration for the Irish heritage. The sentimentality of the song fails to impress Pato, Maureen's friend, who lives outside Ireland like a good number of other westeners of his generation and feels entirely alienated from its narrative: "She does have a creepy oul voice. Always scared me this song did when I was a lad. She's like a ghoul singing. (Pause.) Does the grandmother die at the end, now, or is she just sleeping? ... They don't write songs like that any more. Thank Christ" (23). Pato demonstrates far more interest in singing a popular tune from a movie about a Cadillac and the Yanks inside the house. The various responses of the three to the radio broadcasts reflect their sense of displacement and the corresponding identity confusion.

---

[9] Martin McDonagh, *The Beauty Queen of Leenane* (London: Methuen, 1996), 16. All further references are to this edition.
[10] Una Chaudhuri, op. cit. 3.

Mag insists on her debilitating bodily and mental comfort, symbolized by sitting in her rocking-chair, placed in front of the telly, without reaching out anywhere. For Maureen Ireland is a place with "always someone leaving" (21), herself probably too, in the future. Pato feels wedged between England and Ireland: "when it's there I am, it's here I wish I was ... But I know it isn't here I want to be either" (22). He experiences place as fatefully transitory, and decides on emigration to the United States, like many of his predecessors in Irish literature. Occurring more and more often in (post)modern drama, here too the figure of America can be regarded as central to the disruption of the discourse of home that used to link place and identity.[11]

The television programmes referred to in *The Beauty Queen* are even more inadequate to maintain community feelings and meaningfully organize individual experience. Maureen, at least, expresses her wish to see (the real) Ireland on telly instead of the popular foreign sensational programmes. The latter, however, mesmerize the representative of the younger generation, the frequently cursing nineteen year-old Ray, in whose favourite show "Everybody's always killing each other and a lot of the girls do have swimsuits" (37). This voyeuristic appetite for sex and violent deeds seeks satisfaction in the impersonality of passive media-consumption. In the crucial Scene Six of the play, when Ray should stay on a little longer to hand his brother's love-letter to the forty year-old spinster Maureen, he bursts out complaining: "A whole afternoon I'm wasting here. (Pause.) When I could be at home watching telly" (40). Soon he succumbs to the jealous Mag's persuasions to leave the letter in her hands and departs for home to enjoy the gifts of the box, his undertaken commission not fulfilled. The prospect of entertainment via the screen diverts him from paying attention to the other human being, his addiction being obvious to what Raymond Williams describes as "... a synthetic culture or anti-culture, which is alien to almost everybody, persistently hostile to art and intellectual activity, which it spends much of its time in misrepresenting, and given over to exploiting indifference, lack of feeling, frustration and hatred."[12] In McDonagh's portrayal a fundamental disharmony between the global and the local unfolds, undermining the Leenane people's relations with one another. The media images deployed in the play, ranging from the nostalgically revived traditional home-spun to the onslaught of the shallow cosmopolitan, exemplified by the Australian telly soap, *The Sullivans*, signify a cultural trap that seriously affects the individuals' possibilities for self-fulfilment.

The Spinning Wheel is heard again on the request programme of the radio in the last scene of the play. Chosen by Maureen's sisters to wish many happy

---

[11] Ibid. 6.

[12] Raymond Williams, *Communications* (Harmondworth: Penguin, 1976), 115.

returns on the occasion of their mother's birthday a month before, it sounds most ironical after Mag has been killed by Maureen in an effort to put an end to the past. Even though she has accomplished what Christy Mahon only lied about, it proves too late as she has lost her last hope for finding refuge in returned love. Supposedly, she will not be able to disalign herself from this world of deep-rooted discontents entirely. "The exact fecking image of your mother, you are ..." (60) runs Ray's opinion of her after the funeral. The play concludes with her exit into the hall, but her mother's rocking chair remains very visibly in position, testifying to the weight of personal history and memories. For Maureen the reinvention of the self, advocated by modernity[13] and once liberating Synge's protagonist, is no viable option any more in the context of postmodern chaos. The one-time scandalous word "shift" mentioned in *The Playboy* has its pathetic echo in *The Beauty Queen* when on the morning after a night spent with Pato Maureen comes down to the kitchen wearing only a bra and a slip to indicate her much belated, if ever accomplished, sexual liberation. Christy Mahon's proud look at his promisingly changed self in Pegeen Mike's mirror is ironically parallelled here by Mag's and Maureen's mutual disdain for what the other is, repeating: "Just look at yourself" (33-34). Maureen's detailed story of an imaginary farewell scene between her and Pato, with him "kissing out the window, like they do in films" (51), fails to affect reality in the manner as Christy Mahon's imaginative yarns do. McDonagh's title, *The Beauty Queen of Leenane*, echoes that of Synge, *The Playboy of the Western World* in its grammatical structure, but involves far more irony. Whereas Christy leaves the scene ready for fun and games elsewhere in the company of his magically transformed father, the middle-aged Maureen remains alone and unquestionably not a beauty queen to conquer men's hearts and re-enter the world romping in a renewed guise. In a vacuum, burnt-out as she impresses on the audience, her destiny is probably to face solitude and exile, dislocation from her surroundings as well as from herself.

The Cripple of Inishmaan

The Cripple of Inishmaan (1996) steps back in time to investigate life on Inishmaan, one of the Aran Islands, in 1934. Brian Friel's *Dancing at Lughnasa* (1990), a play taking place in the same historical period as McDonagh's, foregrounds the at times grotesquely dancing body in an unconscious revolt against repression. McDonagh relies on body politics too: his seventeen year-old Cripple Billy, the protagonist of the play, seems construed to embody the distortions and far-reaching traumas of the past underpinning the postcolonial rural community of Inishmaan. However, if Synge can be said

---

13 Homi K. Bhabha, *The Location of Culture* (London: Routledge, 1994), 240.

to have deconstructed "the idea of the Irish peasant carefully assembled by nationalists and the Gaelic League,"[14] McDonagh caricatures what remained left. The *dramatis personae* of *The Cripple* vary between stupidity and violence. The Helen of their small-scale battles and animosities is a lovely faced but shabby-looking teenage girl, who punches men on the nose and breaks eggs on their heads in a grotesque form of self-defence against the ubiquitous danger of lurking abuse. Like Christy Mahon, the crippled playboy of Inishmaan realizes that he is the only truly sensitive person, capable of unselfish love, thrown amidst a bunch of variously limited, ridiculously self-centered and instinctively cruel people who guffaw at him at best: "... patting me on the head like a broken-brained gosawer. The village orphan. The village cripple, and nothing more. Well, there are plenty round here just as crippled as me, only it isn't on the outside it shows."[15]

Synge in *The Playboy* uses a style that represents the peasants' speech as performance, "a critique of attempts at authentic representations—in short, a mimicry of mimesis" revealing "the constructedness of cultural translation."[16] Through this means, the colonial writer subverts the validity of stereotyped imperial approaches to the portrayal of the native Irish. McDonagh has his characters communicate in a language that also calls attention to itself as a product of artistry, creating a liberating discursive space in the wake of Synge. He, however, often replaces the master's lyricism by profanities. Invented as it is, the language of McDonagh's play sounds "hypnotically repetitive, curiously labyrinthine."[17] Combining rural Irish speech with "the edgy street-talk of English cities"[18] it also emphasizes the tendency of our century toward the use of international English.

Depicting a basically oral culture like the world of *The Playboy*, McDonagh has widely divergent versions of a story about the mysterious drowning of Billy's parents circulating among the islanders, with the secret never revealed. On the other hand, as in *The Beauty Queen*, the author includes a mixture of news coming from the wider world to redeem the islanders' inward-looking isolation, but the result proves dubious. When, for instance, Johnnypateenmike and his poteen-drinking, ancient mother discuss an article about Hitler's rise to power in Germany they comment on his "awful

---

14 Christopher Murray, *Twentieth-century Irish Drama: Mirror up to Nation*. (Manchester: Manchester Univ. Press, 1997), 81.
15 Martin McDonagh, *The Cripple of Inishmaan* (London: Methuen, 1997), 66. All further references are to this edition.
16 Gregory Castle, "Staging Ethnography: J. M. Synge's *The Playboy of the Western World* and the Problem of Cultural Transition." *Theatre Journal*, 49.3 (1997), 279.
17 John Russel Taylor, review of *The Cripple of Inishmaan*. *Plays International*, Febr., 1998. 17.
18 Fintan O'Toole, qtd. in: Joseph Feeney, SJ, op cit. 29.

funny moustache" (36-37) and then quickly switch to the far more engaging topic of how Ireland compares with the other nations of the world. The sentence "Ireland mustn't be such a bad place if German fellas want to come to Ireland" (37) and several versions of it using the same pattern with a different subject in the clause keep on recurring in the play to articulate the profound inferiority complex of the for centuries oppressed people. Comical, true, but the joke, as often in Irish culture, balances between surface humour and the deeper, sadder layers of national psychology. Johnnypateenmike himself, with his long nickname mimicking the Irish penchant for wordiness, incarnates a parodistic intersection between the ancient Gaelic *seanchai* and the modern mediaman. He presents the collected local news, mainly petty gossip about accidents and misfortunes, in a measured, bombastic fashion, capitalizing on communal sentiments and a thirst for appealing details, at the same time expecting undivided respect and interest in return.

McDonagh, whose "biggest enthusiasm and expertise is the cinema,"[19] ventures to confront his version of 1930s Irish reality with its contemporary film representation in *The Cripple*. The method parallels Sam Shepard's *True West*, where there are commercially based plans for the renewal of Hollywood images of the mythic American West. McDonagh's play reflects on the circumstances of the shooting of Robert Flaherty's documentary film *Man of Aran* (1934) and then on the finished product itself to inquire into how they affect native experience. The latter, again, is complex for McDonagh: it contains longings, expectations as well as lived reality. First the islanders enthuse over the idea that a film is being made about their life and the younger characters rush to become involved in the enterprise. Their dreams of and wish for a vital change through this, however, soon become thwarted and they come back to harsh reality and get only the film to identify themselves with if they can, but they cannot. Fighting Helen's commentary, for instance, signifies a fundamental discord between the film and individual desire: "I think I might go pegging eggs at the film tomorrow. The Man of Aran me arsehole. 'The Lass of Aran' they could've had, and the pretty lass of Aran. Not some oul shite about thick fellas fecking fishing" (51). 'The Lass of Aran' is, of course, herself, with her frustrated ambitions to become a filmstar, but associates also the 'Lass of Aughrim' of the folksong and together with that the pain and loss Irish people have suffered throughout their history, leading up to the postcolonial grotesqueries magnified by the play.

The Cripple offers a masterful picture of how idealized island-life in Flaherty's *Man of Aran* baffles and even irritates the objects of its mythmaking. Scene Eight of the play has the islanders, in fact actors now taking the role of spectators, watch the film itself. They are seated turned away from the

---

[19] Rupert Christiansen, op. cit. 9.

spectacular sight of rocks and ocean in the background of the stage, as if to further underscore the artificiality of what they view on the screen in the opposite direction. Getting bored, their casual remarks while the film highlights the breathtaking process of catching a big shark by muscled men in a curragh precariously tossed about by huge waves, convey disappointment as well as impatience with such an uninteresting and irrelevant topic:

Mammy	(pause) Ah why don't they just leave the poor shark alone? He was doing no harm.
Johnny	Sure what manner of a story would that be, leaving a shark alone! You want a dead shark.
Bobby	A dead shark, aye or a shark with no ears on him.
Johnny	A dead shark, aye, or a shark kissed a green-teethed girl in Antrim.
Bobby	Do you want a belt, you, mentioning green-teeth girls? (57)

Unarguably, there yawns a wide gap between the islanders' concerns and self-perception and the Hollywood representation that ambitions to provide the world with an 'authentic' story about the true west on the Aran Islands. To include an additional layer of interpretation, it can be mentioned here that apart from the enthusiastic eulogies about its professional merits, the film has elicited criticism for ignoring the social context.[20]

At the expense of a lie about his own impending death, while also tempted by the lustre of the unknown, Billy manages to get to the world of Hollywood film-making when the shooting of *Man of Aran* has finished on the neighbouring island. The plot thickens by undermining both Billy's and the audience's expectations. Presenting him alone and forlorn in a seedy American hotel, Scene Seven of the play leads the audience into the trap of mistaking simulacrum for reality. Next we realize that it has staged a much rehearsed screen test made with Billy in Hollywood. As such, the scene contains a collection of crude images and denuded stereotypes with a potential of jerking tears from the prospective movie-goer for the poor forlorn Irishman dying in exile. It is "the wailing of the banshee" that announces the protagonist's approaching death in the scenario and no "colleen fair to weep" over his soon "still body" (52). In retrospect, Billy himself condemns this manipulative treatment of crippled Irishness: "A rake of shite. And had me singing the fecking 'Croppy Boy' then" (63). In spite of all his efforts, the men of Hollywood decide on employing a healthy actor to play the cripple in their film, the real thing having been found less efficient than the imitation. But Billy's ordeal is not over with this. On coming back, he sincerely reveals his former lie to Bobby, the

---

[20] Cf. Erik Barnouw, *Documentary: A History of the Non-fiction Film.* (Oxford: Oxford Univ. Press, 1993), 98.

boatman whom the story of his incurable illness moved emotionally so as to help him leave for the larger world. However, this only infuriates Bobby who beats Billy up. The scene is strongly reminiscent of the most brutal part of *The Playboy*, where the villagers take revenge on the liar, Christy, because the story of the violent death of his father at his hands has turned out to be false.

Billy does not wish to be away again, because in America he felt unwanted and home is where his own, ironical though this designation may sound, surround him. With a Shavian twist, however, the both self-promoting and Hollywood-invented fiction sadly comes true by the closure of the play: cripple Billy returns home only to die of tuberculosis. Powerless and losing blood, he, again, resembles Christy in appearing as a potential redeemer for the rather hopeless-looking world of Inishmaan. Through the agency of his innate human goodness, he persuades roughneck Helen to accept his invitation to go out walking with him "the way sweethearts be" (78). Brief though the affair may be, it promises to work miracles by infusing some change into the moral destitution of the postcolonial community through love and understanding. In *True West* Shepard opposes "two film scripts and the different imaginative versions of the American West encompassed in them"[21] to demonstrate the mediatedness of reality in the postmodern era. McDonagh, in his turn, suggests a contrast between the distortions of the film and the complex reaching behind the mask that the "wilful, wayward unpredictability of the stage,"[22] exemplified by his play in this case, achieves.

A Skull in Connemara

The two plays forming the second and third parts of *The Lenaane Trilogy*, *A Skull in Connemara* and *The Lonesome West*, both completed in 1997, dramatize a more than ever bleak view of contemporary Irish life in the West. Regarding *A Skull*, the main motifs have their origin, again, in *The Playboy*. Christy's endless boast of hitting the ridge of old Mahon's skull when he raised the loy and fatally "let fall the edge of it,"[23] inspires Synge's villagers to meditate about corpses. At the beginning of Act Three, Jimmy refers to a great variety of skulls on display in the city of Dublin, and Philly recalls his boyhood interest in visiting the graveyard: "... there was a graveyard beyond the house with the remnants of a man who had thighs as long as your arm. He was a horrid man, I'm telling you, and there was many a fine Sunday I'd put

[21] Reingard M. Nischik, "Film as Theme and Technique in Sam Shepard's Plays." *Zeitschrift für Anglistik und Amerikanistik,* 43.1 (1995), 67.
[22] David Hare, "Just what are we playing at?" *The Sunday Times,* 12 Dec., 1993. 11.
[23] J. M. Synge, *The Playboy of the Western World. Collected Works,* Vol. IV. ed. Ann Saddlemeyer (London: Oxford Univ. Press, 1968), 73. All further references are to this edition.

him together for fun ..." (135). The chillingly cryptic conversation throws a grotesque light on the persistent Irish concern with the dead. McDonagh picks up on this, the central scene in his drama being a graveyard where the protagonist, Mick Dowd, digs up skeletons to dispose of them so that new graves can take the place of the old. In the background of *The Playboy* there is a real murder, carried out by the Widow Quin, Christy's more down-to-earth counterpart, who hit her spouse "with a worn pick" (89) resulting in his death by blood poisoning. The motif of the intentional disposal of the spouse is woven into the narrative of *The Skull* too: the process of digging up the old bones turns into an investigation of whether Mick killed his wife, Oona, seven years before.

Although various versions of Oona's death appear in the play, the truth, much in line with McDonagh's postmodern strategy, is never fathomed. His presentation of the closed Western Irish world, however, suggests that in this environment anything can happen. The gravediggers soak in poteen, and the only woman in the play, old Maryjohnny Rafferty, is a frequent visitor to Mick's house to drink his booze and criticise the behaviour of the young. All suffer from moral erosion, an early sign of which is mentioning a television star on the same level with Christ: "Well we can't all be as good as Our Lord. Let alone Eamonn Andrews."[24] As in *The Beauty Queen*, the frequent reference to films and TV shows reinforces the absence of local and national cultural traditions that would allow people to identify with their community. Following the pattern of *The Cripple*, there is mention of another sentimentalizing Hollywood version of Ireland, that of *The Quiet Man* from 1952, directed by John Ford, which sets *The Taming of the Shrew* in an Irish village. The theme of the Dowds' one-time married life in the play is ironically linked to that of the film.

Nurtured on international popular culture and in want of shared values, the characters have no understanding of or patience for each other. They are ready, however, to pepper their exchanges with fierce retorts, which often culminate in farcically nonsensical arguments. For instance, Mick calls insults and insinuations "the self-same thing" (35), which instigates the following:

> Thomas   It's not the self-same thing at all, and if you knew anything about the law then you'd know it's not the self-same thing. So now I have to turn me vague insinuations into something more of an insult, so then we'll all be quits ...

---

[24] Martin McDonagh, *A Skull in Connemara* (London: Methuen, 1997), 5. All further references are to this edition.

Mairtin   (*to* Mick) Your ma was a queer and your da was a queer and
          how they came up with you is a mystery of the Universe! (35-
          36)

What is more, bearing hateful grudges and relentlessly pursuing their selfish
causes, the characters often become infuriated and jump at each other's
throats. The unfolding violent acts derive from and are directed toward the
characters' physical commerce with their immediate environment.[25] For a
start, Thomas, the guard shoves his younger brother, Mairtin, Mick's half-
witted assistant in digging, down into an open grave, giving himself and Mick
the opportunity to have a good laugh and kick mud on the youngster's body. In
general, the latter is slow to notice the various dirty tricks the adults play on
him, taking him as the clown of the village.

   The laughter McDonagh undoubtedly provokes, carries with it
embarrassing effects. The play resonates with the smashing of skulls,
belonging to both the living and the dead, in words as well as in actual deeds.
Both Mick and Thomas hit Mairtin on the head, the one for his getting the rose
locket from Oona's neck after the theft of the corpse, and the other for the
boy's revealing to Mick that his brother was behind the premature removal.
Between the two blows, the absurdity involved is reinforced visually as the re-
entry of Mairtin on stage with *"a big bloody crack down the centre of his
forehead, dripping onto his shirt"* (58) hilariously echoes old Mahon's
crawling back on all fours in Synge's last act. Thomas, who had stolen Oona's
remains out of the grave before Mick got there, was seen by Mairtin carving a
hole in the skull to fabricate evidence with which to prove the suspected
murder. The corrupt plan forms part of his self-servicing ambitions: he craves
for promotion and dreams about successfully investigating the most weird
cases like Petrocelli. The climax comes when Mick and Mairtin, both fairly
drunk, shatter skulls and bones to smithereens with their mallets. It is their
rage and frustration that fuel this finely orchestrated scene in the drama, with
the two enacting their ability to cope with the remnants of the past only
through aggressive destruction, "... the only lesson skulls be understanding"
(43).

   The failure to relate to the past differently combined with the drive to
prove their own points at the expense of the truth manifests itself also in the
(feigned) amnesia of the characters. Mairtin attributes his skull-injury received
from Mick to drink-driving, which saves the man from being arrested by
Thomas. Thus the boy can continue indulging in his contempt for his brother

---

[25] Cf. what is written about violence in Edward Bond's plays in Stanton B. Garner, Jr.,
Bodied Spaces: Phenomenology and Performance in Contemporary Drama (Ithaca: Cornell
Univ. Press, 1994), 178.

as a bad cop. Creating a powerful stage image at the end of the play, Mick "...
*picks up the skull and stares at it a while, feeling the forehead crack. He rubs
the skull against his cheek, trying to remember"* (66). His gentle caressing of
the skull embodies an adequately grotesque closure to the play, a black comedy
presenting various attempts to conceal and reveal details about the past,
whichever fits the never fully charted individual scenario.

The Lonesome West

The Lonesome West takes its title from *The Playboy*, where in Act One
Michael James, holding up the coat of the escaping Shawn, bombastically de-
claims with an amount of irony: "Oh, there's sainted glory this day in the lonesome west ..." (65). McDonagh appropriates the phrase to further contest the
national narrative about the West of Ireland, which dates back to the early
post-independence days when "... with a border truncating the country, the
image of the creative unity of the west, the vision of heroic rural life in the
Gaeltacht ... served as metaphor of social cohesion and an earnest of the cultural unity that transcended class politics and history."[26] In accordance with
his works being informed by place-as-identity, McDonagh calls for critical
contextualization in the representation of myths about another West, that of
America. Concerning these related myths Luke Gibbons' seminal study claims
that

> For all their similarities as foundational myths—sharing agrarian ideals, an
> aversion to law and order and to the centralization of the state—it is the dif-
> ferences between them that are most striking. The wild west is an outpost of
> individualism, extolling the virtues of the self-made man that lie at the heart of
> the American dream. By contrast, the recourse to the west in Ireland is im-
> pelled by a search for community, a desire to escape the isolation of the self
> and to immerse oneself in the company of others.[27]

Shepard's *True West* negates the existence of a true American west, symboliz-
ing the loss of individual freedom and heroism by the cowboy figure in a state
of living death.[28] As for the myth of the west being the centre of Irish communal values, in *The Playboy* the western community still fullfils the function
of promoting the individual although in a way pointing toward demytholo-

[26] Terence Brown, *Ireland: A Social and Cultural History 1922-85* (London: Fontana Press,
1990), 92.
[27] Luke Gibbons, *Transformations in Irish Culture* (Notre Dame, Indiana: Univ. of Notre
Dame Press in association with Field Day, 1996), 13.
[28] Megan Williams, "Nowhere Man and the Twentieth-Century Cowboy: Images of Identity
and American History in Sam Shepard's *True West.*" *Modern Drama*, 40.1 (1997), 63.

gization. Christy renews his identity and leaves as "a likely gaffer" (173) through contact with as well as in spite of the westerners who castigate and viciously try to lynch him. *The Lonesome West* subverts the myth entirely, presenting a community, that of Leenane, where suicides are piled on top of homicides and the traditional value of Catholicism is interpreted by the murderer in the following way: "It's always the best ones go to hell. Me, probably straight to heaven I'll go, even though I blew the head off poor dad. So long as I go confessing to it anyways. That's the good thing about being Catholic. You can shoot your dad in the head and it doesn't even matter at all."[29] And this in the presence of the customary crucifix on the wall. The other protagonist collects cheap saints' figurines, only to be destroyed by his brother during a quarrel. Father Welsh, an onstage character here, can merely repeat the clichés of religion imploringly without any tangible effect, his day-to-day frustrations urging him to confess that the community has had a destructive effect on him. The one-time value of sidestepping the law is turned upside down too, crime can flourish because of the acknowledged weakness of the authorities.

Portraying the fraternal hostility of the two main characters who share a home, the setting of the play renders this world more claustrophobic than ever in McDonagh. Like Shepard's Aston and Lee, McDonagh's brother figures, Coleman and Valene in *The Lonesome West* are complementary figures, with neither of the two better than the other: between the two of them they have broken all the major commandments. Coleman shot their father dead for virtually nothing and Valene forced his brother to sign the inheritance over to him for his complicity in hushing up the deed. While the pair of Aston and Lee embodies the division in the individual American psyche, the conflict between McDonagh's brother figures signals an essentially intra-community one, restaging what has already happened between other people. With fights repeatedly flaring up between them, the vicious restlessness of this "odd" couple enacts the pervasive hateful tensions within their larger environment. However, the comedy is not missing even from this. In a both immensely amusing and deadly sinister scene they "attempt to make up, apologising to each other for past misdeeds" which escalates into a "competition as to who can confess to the worst crime,"[30] turning the Irish storytelling tradition inside out. It is not long, however, before they murderously attack each other again.

Both Coleman and Valene are middle-aged bachelors, whose chief pastime is going over to the pub or reading women's magazines, the articles of which

[29] Martin McDonagh, *The Lonesome West* (London: Methuen, 1997), 53-54. All further references are to this edition.
[30] Robert Tanitch, review of *The Leenane Trilogy. Plays and Players*, Oct., 1997. 7.

satisfy their adolescent-like needs concerning the other sex they seem never to have known closely. Most grotesquely, though touching human events surround them, Coleman and Valene keep on being reminded of characters and incidents from various films and television shows. The synthetic culture carries unbridled attraction for them, since it covers the miserable tragedies, both physical and moral, of their life and that of the whole town. Discussing the local policeman's suicide with the priest, Valene ponders: "So Tom'll be in hell now, he will? ... I wonder if he's met the fellow from *Alias Smith and Jones* yet? Ah, that fellow must be old be now. Tom probably wouldn't even recognise him. That's if he saw *Alias Smith and Jones* at all. I only saw it in England. It mightn't have been on telly here at all" (26). The pieces of news about the larger world they have access to through their magazines interest them only in so far as they strike some familiar sensational note. From *Take a Break* Valene picks out about the war-tormented Balkans: "There's a lad here in Bosnia and not only has he no arms but his mammy's just died. (*Mumbles as he reads, then*): Ah they're only after fecking money, the same as ever" (45). Such details in *The Lonesome West*, while spotlighting the limitations of the brothers' personal interests, also expose the superficiality of the magazine treatment of devastating problems and conflicts in the world, likely to foster the desensitization of their readers to local issues.

As for love and tenderness, the budding of it remains buried in shameful side glances and immature and incomplete attempts at expressing emotions. Father Welsh and Girleen, a tamer though not less virgin-whore version of Helen in *The Cripple,* sit together in an early scene and almost understand each other. Rough as she is on the surface, Girleen perceives happiness as a goal in life when meditating on the community of the dead in the cemetery. However, the man of the Church cannot think of a self-renewing relationship with the girl who pines for him in vain and sheds buckets of tears at his funeral. Even the sacrificial scalding of his own hands to separate the local Cain and Abel and his subsequent suicide fail to redeem the surrounding moral vacuum. Leenane remains, Welsh himself concludes, "the murder capital of fecking Europe" (34), which sounds highly sarcastic set beside the reference to the EC in the play.

Conclusion

Blending innocence with brutality and stretching both to the absurdly ridiculous at times, McDonagh's is a theatre where the underside of rural life is shamelessly laid bare in its self-destructiveness, undermining the traditional identification of the West as the heart of the nation and national identity. Nevertheless, in tune with the postmodern it refuses to encourage the reader to abstract or translate what it offers[31] as a re-presentation of Irishness. What it constitutes, in my interpretation, is a possible world that contains an undesirable alternative state of the actual[32] to exorcize the still lurking demons of colonial distortions and to expose the alienating influences of the present. On the other hand, McDonagh's inclusion of images from several cultural and literary works beside his own enhances the awareness of the audience that his is also only a kind of view. The strategy can best be comprehended in terms of Homi K. Bhabha's theory which stresses that "the postcolonial prerogative seeks to affirm and extend a new collaborative dimension, both within the margins of the nation-space and across boundaries between nations and peoples" that can result in achieving "the postmodern from the position of the postcolonial."[33] And this is exactly what establishes the uniqueness of McDonagh on the contemporary Irish scene.

A complex approach reveals that McDonagh does not only dismantle and deconstruct. Through the enriched theatricality and well measured, never overwritten text of his plays he shocks us "with a twist in the tail," deploying "myths and images to challenge and transform the status quo."[34] His drama deviates from the literariness and lyricism of Friel or the reconciliation achieved in Murphy that are more apt to call certain forms of revivalist drama back to mind, and invites comparison with the writing of the post-revival demythologizers and iconoclasts.

---

[31] See Steven Connor, "Postmodern Performance." *Postmodernist Culture: An Introduction to Theories of the Contemporary* (New York: Basil Blackwell, 1989), 141.
[32] Cf. M. L. Ryan's catalogue of types of alternative possible worlds qtd. in: Elena Semino, "Possible Worlds in Poetry." *Journal of Literary Semantics,* 25.3 (1996), 192.
[33] Homi K. Bhabha, op. cit. 175.
[34] Richard Kearney, *Postnationalist Ireland: Politics, Culture, Philosophy.* (London: Routledge, 1997), 123.

Part Two

Individual and Gender Identity

Alternative Articulations of Female Subjectivity and Gender Relations in Contemporary Irish Women's Plays: The Example of Marina Carr

Introduction

Parallel to the development of drama by women in other Western countries, female voices in the Irish theatre have, from the 1970s onwards, made themselves more conspicuous than ever before. However, the conditions for their work are still influenced by the constraints of the postcolonial consciousness, as both Catholic and Protestant ideologies put pressure on women "to retain the domestic role as their primary function."[1] In the whole island there is a rapid moving away from old patterns in social, religious and gender relations, yet it takes time for the result of this to become a direct shaping force on day-to-day human interaction. Contemporary drama by women, not necessarily to be labelled as feminist, challenges the stereotypes rampant in Irish thinking about women and about the context that largely determines their lives. On the side of form, their work tends to resist the perpetuation of realistic conventions "not only to thwart the illusion of 'real' life, but also … to threaten the patriarchal ideology imbedded in 'story'" and use a different discursive strategy to address women's issues.[2]

As colonial Ireland suffered the implementation of double standards and distortion of facts for centuries, its culture became imbued with various forms of the non-realistic and evasive to cope with and to spiritually transcend the oppressive situation. Therefore, according to several interpretations, the fantastic has become a salient feature of Irish drama be it of male or female authorship. With more general relevance, Patrick D. Murphy claims that the fantastic as "a perceptual orientation rather than a structural one; a way of getting at significant cultural and psychological issues … unamenable to realistic methods of writing and representation" often functions in drama to reveal "the deeper, unconscious sources of identity."[3] For Irish women playwrights this mode and, in a broader sense, the violation of realistic codifying and the use of indirect approaches serve as most appropriate tools to achieve alterna-

---

[1] Anna McMullan, "Irish women playwrights since 1958." Trevor R. Griffiths and Margaret Llewellyn-Jones (eds.), *British and Irish Women Dramatists Since 1958: A Critical Handbook* (Buckingham: Open University Press, 1993), 111.
[2] Jeanie Fort, "Realism, Narrative, and the Feminist Playwright—A Problem of Reception." Helene Keyssar (ed.), *Feminist Theatre and Theory* (London: Macmillan, 1996), 21-22.
[3] Patrick D. Murphy (ed.), "Introduction." *Staging the Impossible. The Fantastic Mode in Modern Drama* (Westport, Connecticut: Greenwood, 1992), 3, 10.

tive subject positioning as well as to rechannel audience expectations. What further distinguishes their work is its bold scrutiny of established notions of gender identity and a sensitive reconstruction of female subjectivity while evoking new possibilities for self-assertion. At the same time, they naturally draw from the heritage of the folk imagination, myths, religion, and also from the visionary and magic qualities informing both the oral and literary traditions of Ireland.

Low in the Dark

The plays of Midlands-reared writer Marina Carr (1964-) are widely acclaimed for their innovative stretching of the boundaries of dramatic inquiry and enriching the scope of themes. Her first play, *Low in the Dark* (1989), orchestrates scenes in a non-realistic mode that even verges on the absurd, indebted to Beckett (especially to *Waiting for Godot* and *What Where*) as Anthony Roche contends.[4] Yet what Carr persistently explores here is the complexities of male/female attitudes and gendered preconceptions, using multiple role-playing as her primary device. At the play's opening, Bender and Binder, mother and daughter are introduced, the fiftyish Bender giving birth again and Binder undertaking the nursing of the new baby. The suggested continuity of this process emphasises the stereotyping of generations of women by the connected roles of giving birth to and looking after children. Re-reading them through the female imagination, the play also deconstructs elements of male behaviour. Binder takes the part of the male who brings a bunch of flowers for his wife (here played by Bender), but remains interested solely in his own domestic comfort and ignores the pain the woman endures when giving birth. The language bridging the two genders is exposed in a game about romantic love-confession, caricaturing not only the clichéd vocabulary of lovers, but also the expectation of hearing the words again and again though their meaninglessness is well known.

The other pair of characters in the drama, the males Baxter and Bone, try out traditional female functions, enacting scenarios in which one of them wears a necklace and looks pregnant. Underscoring the social constructedness, performativity and inherent ambiguity of the most widely accepted gender roles, the unfolding chain of reversals shows the "normal" in the cracked mirror of gender divisions. A notable parallel and possible influence in the domain of feminist drama can be detected in Caryl Churchill's *Cloud Nine* (1979), where cross-gender casting harshly satirises the Victorian denaturalisation of the characters' individuality. By alienating iconicity, as Elin Diamond

---

[4] Anthony Roche, *Contemporary Irish Drama from Beckett to McGuinness*. (Dublin: Gill and Macmillan, 1994), 287.

describes Churchill's strategy, "the ideology of gender is exposed and thrown back to the spectator."[5] In Carr, the process is continually interrupted by the characters falling out of their adopted behaviour to enhance and further ironise the overall effect. The technique incorporates also a subtle commentary on how both males and females are obsessed with, as well as mystified by, gendered otherness, reconstructing it in a way that echoes their dreams and private needs. The expectations assume fantastic proportions when expressing the wish to have the other fulfill both a set of conventional roles and perform gender-bending at the same time:

> BONE   I want a woman who knows how to love. I want lazer beams
>   coming out of her eyes when I enter the room. I want her to knit
>   like one possessed. I want her to cook softly.
> BINDER I want a man who'll wash my underwear, one who'll brush my
>   hair, one who'll talk before, during and after. I want a man
>   who'll make other men look mean.[6]

The issue of gender is so ubiquitous in *Low in the Dark*, that the fifth character, called Curtains and referred to as a woman, embodies and re-negotiates views of and attitudes to the female. Her lack of distinctive human traits, because neither her face, nor other parts of her body are seen during the play, foregrounds the nature of the male gaze that tends to de-realise the woman into an object of mystery, negating the value of individuality. Constructed "as a site/sight of 'looking-at-being-looked-at-ness' in performance," she appears bodily "under-displayed,"[7] attracting attention by her neutral physicality. Her closed curtains are supposed to conceal something exciting, by which means Carr both signifies and subverts the exclusion of women from representation.[8] Pointing to women's obvious desire for a change, the two female protagonists angrily insist on Curtains' revealing herself:

> BINDER *(Yelling after her).* Open those bloody curtains!
> BENDER I'd love to rip them off her! There is life to be lived, I'd say as
>   I'd rip them off, or didn't you hear? (67)

But it is not possible for her to comply with these demands, and she remains locked in the folds like the other women in their own ambiguous situation.

---

[5] Elin Diamond, *Unmaking Mimesis: Essays on Feminism and Theatre* (London: Routledge, 1997) 46.

[6] Marina Carr, *Low in the Dark*. David Grant (ed.), *New Irish Plays* (London: New Hern Books, 1990), 77. All further references are to this edition.

[7] Elaine Aston, *An Introduction to Feminism and Theatre* (London: Routledge, 1995), 94.

[8] Cf. Anna McMullan, op. cit. 118.

Curtains is also the storyteller of the play, which begins and concludes with bits of her habitual narration about a man and a woman having a mutual dream then roaming the earth in a rhythm of meeting and drawing apart. At first this seems to work as a cliché which stresses the female interest in fantasising about and discussing intersexual relations, supported by Bender's and Binder's eagerness to contribute and feeling specially thrilled on hearing that the man and woman in the story have fallen in love. Gradually, the preoccupation turns out to be, however, the telling of "the tale,"[9] the archetypal story of man and woman finding, then losing, yet again seeking each other. Crisscrossing the interrupted and resumed fragments of the narrative, repetitions and absurd twists perform the variations on basically the same encompassing theme of humankind since the dawn of time: "The millions of men turned to the millions of women and said, 'I'll not forget you.' The millions of women turned and answered, 'I'll not forget you either.' And so they parted" (140).

Itself disjointed, the main narrative line about everyman and everywoman travelling together branches out into stories within stories, as in traditional Irish storytelling. They recapitulate the experiences occuring in the course of life, with a joint echo of the Beckettian tragicomic and the Brechtian parabolic, for instance in the following section:

> So the man and the woman walked, not speaking unless spoken to, which was never as neither spoke. Going along the path in this amiable fashion they came upon a woman singing in a ditch. 'Sing us your song,' the man said. The woman sang.
>
> > In Salamanca I mislaid my daughter,
> > In Carthage they killed my son,
> > In Derry I lost my lover,
> > In this ditch I've lost my mind.
>
> 'You've ruined our day,' the man said. 'Don't be so cruel,' the woman said and turning to the woman in the ditch, she asked, 'Is there anything we can do except help you?' The woman did not reply. So the man and the woman hit her and moved on. (96-97)

In *Happy Days* the man Shower or Cooker and his female companion look down at Winnie stuck in her hole, but the sight inspires them only to show more concern with themselves. Similarly, Carr's interfering couple attack the destitute woman in the ditch out of sheer self-pity. According to the conventional ideas about female gentle-heartedness, the woman's initial utterances present her as being more compassionate; however, the outcome of the inset story satirises the inward-looking egotism of both of them. The scene seems to be complicated, moreover, by the suggestion that the woman's behaviour takes

---

[9] Anthony Roche, op. cit. 288.

this turn probably as a result of her blind submission to male leadership. Welding intertextuality and dramatic self-reflexivity, Carr's use of Curtains in the role of the female *seanchai* contributes to the revelation of the nature of man-woman relations and gender roles that *Low in the Dark* is endlessly playing with.

The Mai

Carr's *The Mai* (1994) includes seven females who represent four generations of women in a family; they are referred to as the "Connemara click" by Robert, the only male in the drama.[10] The unfolding of the main character, the Mai's renewal and then fatal crisis of marriage, which constitutes the plot itself, is presented in a refashioned form of the memory play. Its central narrator is Millie, the Mai's daughter, who, after many years, feels she is being haunted by "that childhood landscape," the "dead silent world that tore our hearts out for a song" (71). Replacing conventional dramatic logic, it is through visual effects and a cluster of narratives that character and internal action become elucidated in the play. It opens and closes on Millie's evocation of the image of the Mai looking out of the window on Owl Lake, beside which she has a house built to win her husband back. However, her efforts are rewarded only briefly. The difference in the views of the two of the matrimonial relationship is visualised in corporeal terms. At the beginning of the drama the musician Robert's playing the cello bow across The Mai's breasts testifies to his male vision which reverts the female body "to an image not of itself, but its (male) cultural articulation."[11] After he has rejected her, she plays herself with the same bow, attempting to recuperate her embodiment as a female subject who desires attention and love for what she is. The Mai's disappointment in love ends with suicide, a fate which is shown powerfully linked with both the spirit of the place invested with human aspirations and the history of women in her family.

Millie's story in Act One about the origin of Owl Lake from the legendary Coillte's tears, shed over change in love and about her subsequent dissolution in the water once her lover joined "the dark witch of the bog" (42) anticipates the Mai's death. The *"ghostly lit"* (42) haunting memory of the tragedy is reinforced when The Mai's drowned body appears in her husband's arms concluding the same scene. Framed by the window, the symbolic threshold of two contrasting worlds, nature and the distorting social mores, the picture seems

---

10 Marina Carr, *The Mai* (Loughcrew, Oldcastle: The Gallery Press, 1995), 66. All further references are to this edition.

11 Stanton B. Garner, Jr., *Bodied Spaces: Phenomenology and Performance in Contemporary Drama* (Ithaca and London: Cornell Univ. Press, 1994), 187.

like an ironic reversal of the Madonna with the dead Redeemer. Carr's disruption of the linearity of the play's narrative line precipitating "non-mimetic shifts of subject, scene, and language"[12] represents the associative structure of the female experience. The interpenetration of the old story and the modern predicament re-inscribes the personal in the archaic, stressing the mysterious roots of subjectivity.

Mediating a variety of feelings and responses deeply carved in the memory of generations of women, the other stories, presented in the Irish fashion with a relish for verbal embellishments, are about love, happy dreams as well as loss and suffering. They give voice to the female characters' need for the absolute, the whole, countering the drabness of mundane reality. Commenting on some crucial implications of her work Carr stated in an interview that "It's an inbuilt mechanism in every individual to want the extraordinary, the unreachable, the impossible."[13] Couched in a story which echoes Curtain's rendering of the archetypal meetings and departures of the male and female in *Low in the Dark*, the Mai's dream the night before her wedding yearns for such transcendence, set against the prospect of doom:

> At the bend in the river I see you coming towards me whistling through two leaves of grass ... and you pass me saying, Not yet, not yet, not for thousands and thousands of years. And I turn to look after you and you're gone and the river is gone and away in the distance I see a black cavern and I know it leads to nowhere and I start walking that way because I know I'll find you there. (26)

Combining reality and elements of fairy tales, a beautiful story, related by Millie as she had heard it from her mother, brings The Mai together with a little princess, reinforcing the pull of the dream world. The two of them met while the Mai was spending time in England fund-raising, to be able to have her house built by the mysterious lake, the materially determined circumstances thus heightening the hunger for the magic:

> ... The Mai and the princess were two of a kind, moving towards one another across deserts and fairytales and years till they finally meet in a salon under Marble Arch and waltz around enthralled with one another and their childish impossible world. Two little princesses on the cusp of a dream, one five, the other forty. (46)

---

[12] Donald E. Morse, "'Sleepwalkers along a Precipice': Staging memory in Marina Carr's *The Mai." The Hungarian Journal of English and American Studies* 2.2 (1996), 113.
[13] Heidi Stephenson and Natasha Langridge, *Rage and Reason: Women Playwrights on Playwriting* (London: Methuen, 1997), 147.

Foregrounding movement through the medium of dance that links body and soul in harmony, the story asserts the potential for the re-appropriation of wholeness through reunion with childhood dreams, some pre-Oedipal state of being in the world of the Kristevan semiotic. As The Mai later recalls, her own mother also cherished the wish "to be a child again" (70), and freely wade in the river Sruthán na mBláth with the golden sand underneath. The little Arab princess had her fate arranged for her already, being betrothed to a much older man of both affluence and authority. Yet in her dazzling though delimiting environment, the self-reliant Mai must have carried for her a profound vision of alterity.

Like *Low in the Dark*, *The Mai* is also endowed with a character who appears to own mythic power and condenses female qualities in one person, as a larger-than-life "mixture of the naturalistic and the *cailleach* from folklore."[14] She is the one hundred year-old Grandma Fraochlán, whose story about the love of her husband, the nine-fingered fisherman who swam miles to arrive in her bedchamber "his skin a livid purple from tha freezin' sea" (69) stresses the power of sexuality in "re-making the Woman."[15] She even dances with the air as a way of self-celebration after quoting her husband who used to call her "Queen a th'ocean" (22). Remembering her own unmarried mother, who chose the name "The Duchess" for herself and invented fantastic stories of how the Sultan of Spain, the father of her daughter will come for them, Grandma voices the richness of dreams opposing the emptiness of the real. Her exotic, Irish and Eastern origin contributes to her "matrilineal line of support" with which she manages to connect the community of women in the drama "more fully to a sense of their own identity."[16] However, this heritage contains the danger of cherishing too high expectations, as The Mai keenly feels: "... her stories made us long for something extraordinary to happen in our lives. I wanted my life to be huge and heroic and pure as in the days of yore, my prince at my side, and together we'd leave our mark on it" (55).

Creating a mysterious atmosphere not unlike the one in Yeats's "The Wild Swans at Coole," the realm of nature is represented by the sounds of swans and geese to offset the human world in the drama. Since in Irish folklore swans are known to be loyal to their mates till death, the frequent references to sighting this bird serve as background to the overpowering desire of The Mai for the restoration of mutual love in marriage. Nonetheless, it is also through exam-

---

[14] Christopher Murray, *Twentieth-century Irish drama: mirror up to nation* (Manchester: Manchester Univ. Press, 1997), 237.

[15] Elaine Aston, op. cit. 50.

[16] Anthony Roche, "Woman on the Threshold: J. M. Synge's *The Shadow of the Glen*, Teresa Deevy's *Katie Roche* and Marina Carr's *The Mai*." *Irish University Review* 25.1 (1995), 159.

ples from nature that she perceives and learns to understand unavoidable loss and impending finality. A story of Millie's describes how the keening of a female swan at the death of a cob once transfixed her at the window with "a high haunting sound ... you hope never to hear again and it's a sound you know you will" (51).

Engendering as well as remythologising the old Irish dilemma of being trapped between dreams and reality in The Mai's precarious condition, Carr concludes the drama with her suicide as a form of re-writing fate. Declining to accept living among fragments like the other women, The Mai chooses the kind of action available to preserve her integrity and realign herself with nature rather than remain a split-minded victim of Robert's treatment which is prone to render her passive, dead before actual death, while making her an object of hostile social judgement.

Portia Coughlan

The self-chosen death of a woman is the resolution of Carr's *Portia Coughlan* (1996) as well. Here the most important non-realistic device is the use of the double, in the figure of the central character Portia's twin brother, Gabriel, who drowned himself in the Belmont river. Gabriel's ghost haunts Portia: aware of his presence and hearing his songs she has the irresistable desire to walk along the river and think of him, her "true being, her suffering self... bound up in dreams."[17] What torments her is the feeling of incompleteness, the lack of something vitally important: "He woulda bin thirty taday as well ... sometimes ah thinche on'y half a'me is left, the worst half ..."[18] Carr acknowledges that the names Portia and Belmont are borrowed from Shakespeare's *The Merchant of Venice* (311), thus demonstrating how the greatest playwright of the English-speaking world haunts the author herself.

The dead but for Portia mysteriously living Gabriel represents what she misses in her environment: the poetry of the unknown and the right of the boundless working of the imagination. In contrast, life with Raphael, her husband, demands that Portia serves her family, promotes the three children's socialisation and boosts his business interests. The tension between the two forces is performed by the symbolic confrontation of two objects in the very first scene of the drama. Portia puts Raphael's birthday present, a vulgar-looking though obviously very expensive diamond bracelet, the sign of material advancement, out of sight, and keeps glancing at the box that holds the twins' one-time secret treasures, freshly pulled out of the river. Often the

---

[17] Christopher Murray, op. cit. 238.

[18] Marina Carr, *Portia Coughlan*. Frank McGuinness (ed.): *The Dazzling Dark: New Irish Plays* (London: Faber and Faber, 1996), 258. All further references are to this edition.

drama stages the sister in her living room and the dead brother at the river-
bank simultaneously, Portia's attentiveness to what is beyond the surface of
things and his singing emphasising their mysterious closeness.

The story of the Belmont river in *Portia Coughlan* incorporates elements
of folktale and myth. Related by the protagonist herself, it describes the origin
of the river connected to a woman's suffering caused by human cruelty and
then healed by the balancing forces of nature:

> ... she had the power a'tellin' tha future.... tha people 'roun' these parts
> grew aspicious of her acause everthin' she perdicted happened. Tha began to
> belave thah noh on'y was she perdictin', buh causin', all a' thim terrible
> things to chome abouh. So wan nigh' tha impaled her an a stache wheer tha
> river now is, mayhap righ' here, an' tha left her ta die. Ud's a slow deah,
> cruel an' mos' painful an' for nights an' nights ya could hare her tormintid
> groanin. Bel, tha valla god heerd her, an' her cries near druv him mad. He
> could noh unnerstan' how her people could treah her so for she war wan
> a'thim, on'y a little different. He chem down tha valla in a flood a' rage, cov-
> erin' houses an' livestoche an' churches over, an' tooche tha ghirl in hees
> arms, down, down, all the way down ta tha mouh a' th'Atlantich. (267)

Portia's outcast fate and death in the river are encapsulated by the legend, as in
the case of *The Mai*. The physical torture the girl of mysterious, Cassandra-
like powers faces in it is equalled in the play proper by the crippling narrow-
mindedness and lack of attention that surround Portia. She throws herself into
the river to meet her shadow self, Gabriel, thus escaping the torment of living
with a sense of incompleteness and foresight of death and doom threatening
her children in such a world. Disillusionment with the fulfilling potential of
sexual pleasures with men who are not willing to listen adds to her dissatisfac-
tion and unrest, rekindling her uncommonly strong love for her twin brother.
It is not an incest motif though, according to Carr, but like "one of the oldest
stories of what the world was born out of, a brother and sister, well, the
Greek world, with the tale of Bibylus in Ovid's *Metamorphoses*, where the
sister falls in love with her brother."[19]

Recalling Yeats's lovers Dectora and Forgael in *The Shadowy Waters*
(1911), Portia and Gabriel had tried, as children, to sail out on the sea in a
boat "'jus anawheers thah's noh here'" (275), unafraid of anything. The adult
Portia's choice to join Gabriel by leaving the world of everyday duties and
bonds displays further echoes of Yeats, in whose drama the supernatural often
confronts the real, inviting us to perceive "experience as dialectic."[20] In *The
Land of Heart's Desire* (1894) Mary's temptation by the Faery Child to go

---

[19] Heidi Stephenson and Natasha Langridge, op. cit. 152.
[20] Christopher Murray, op. cit. 18.

with her away from family life and married love prefigures the dilemma of Carr's protagonist. The role of a legend encapsulating the fulfilment of fate is also shared by the two plays: in Yeats's drama Mary, before the arrival of the Faery Child, reads about a princess of old times who heard "A voice singing on a May Eve like this, / And followed, half awake and half asleep, / Until she came into the Land of Faery."[21]

There are mythical beliefs about twins being "transformed salmon" that "may not go near water, lest they should be changed back again into the fish."[22] Portia refers to the salmon's ever-renewed wandering and joins the re-transformed Gabriel and the river, their real terrain of living. Contemporary Irish literature frequently deploys the figure of the double in various forms, as part of its project to revise the manifold issue of identity. The loss of a twin brother features also in a novel by female writer Deirdre Madden, titled *Hidden Symptoms* (1986), where the setting is Troubles-riven Belfast. Theresa, the surviving sister feels as if imprisoned after the violent death of Francis, her twin, which is suggested "again and again with the same images: a wall, a pit, a hole"[23] —in a way comparable to Portia's feeling that their house resembles a 'coffin' (255). Having to live without Francis shakes Theresa's faith in both God and people and, like Portia, she wishes she had died with him. The haunting memory of the dead twin becomes metaphorical of the sense of fragmentation as a still vivid element of the postcolonial Irish psyche.

The chronological reversal Carr deploys in *Portia* places the whole Act Two after the suicide, while Act Three presents what took place on the day preceding it. "Playing with time" interests her, the author claims, and "after-knowledge of an event that is about to take place always ups the ante."[24] Again, Caryl Churchill can be quoted as a predecessor in this respect: *Top Girls* notably reverses the order of the last two scenes. Its closing word, uttered by Angie, the teenage girl, refers to her anxiety, which resonates with presentiment of trouble while highlighting in retrospect the enormity of the neglectful behaviour of Marlene, the mother, who builds her career sacrificing family life. In Carr's drama, the scenes of Act Three provide the audience with subtle clues to the protagonist's psychic confusion pushing her toward the final decision.

Portia suffers more and more from a guilty conscience because of the failure of the one-time plan to commit suicide together with Gabriel, when she suddenly grew afraid and let him wade ahead in the water alone. His singing

[21] William Butler Yeats, *Collected Plays* (London: Macmillan, 1982 [1934]), 55.

[22] James Frazer, *The Golden Bough* (Ware, Hertfordshire: Wordsworth Editions, 1993), 66.

[23] Deirdre Madden, *Hidden Symptoms* (London: Faber and Faber, 1988), 49.

[24] Heidi Stephenson and Natasha Langridge, op. cit. 154.

now appears to her not at a distance as in Act One but closer and closer, parallel with her strengthening alienation from those around her while her inner split is becoming wider. She can hardly speak about anything else but Gabriel and herself, in the vain hope of sharing the weight of psychic hell with others. Her mother proves particularly uncomprehending, since her sole interest lies in keeping to the demands of the external order with its clear-cut standards to govern decent womanly behaviour. Seeing just the madness of her daughter's obsession with the ghost, it is to be treated, according to her, much like the Cassandra-minded girl in the story about the river: "An' ah'd say yar nex' stop'll be th'asylum, ah'd have ya comihhed on'y ah don't want ana more blood an me hands" (303).

In the very last scene of the play Portia makes one last desperate effort to explain herself to her husband, urged by the need to be fully honest about what so deeply affects her. But her story of how close she has always felt to Gabriel and how they made love as children horrifies Raphael: "Ah've long suspected whah ya toult me abouh you an' Gabriel. An' ah don' know whah ta say anamore Portia. Ah don' know ya ah all" (307). He is just of the earth, without the superhuman ability to forgive and forget all and redeem as well as liberate Portia from her deeply felt division with the power of love and understanding. She then cannot but choose suicide, the unity with her other half, as the only way to reconfirm her autonomous selfhood. This done in the face of the demand to go on living for the sake of her children, the play subverts one of the most sanctified patriarchal beliefs about the obligation of women. At the same time, through Portia's mysterious yearning for her double, it re-situates the female self as the bearer of the contemporary problem of people feeling torn between day-to-day responsibilities and the call of an overshadowed, atavistic side of life. In the context of Ireland's rapid material development, the gap reveals itself as one between postmodern crudities and the attachment to a more attractive, because emotionally grounded and aesthetically varied past.

By the Bog of Cats

Entitled *By the Bog of Cats* (1998), the latest play written by Carr is set in a bogland. Since Seamus Heaney's famous bog-poems we are aware that this synechdoche for Ireland herself harbours dark secrets and mysteries. Told by a supernatural, folk tradition figure called the Catwoman who is the keeper of the place, the central story of the drama joins the fate of a black swan and the similarly named Hester Swane, the protagonist. As in Irish mythology, the bird incarnates the soul, its death by freezing entailing the end of the woman due to another kind of chill, that of the heart of her man toward her. The story itself involves Hester's off-stage mother, a restless tinker whom people thought too strange and dangerous to live among them. According to the

Catwoman, she put her newborn "in the black swan's lair,"[25] probably to have her become nature's child like herself. Forty year-old Hester is a woman of deep longing, left alone by her mother for whom she never stops waiting. Emotionally wounded like the Mai, she cannot bear the thought of being metaphorically "flung on the ashpit" (55) by her one-time lover, just because he wants to start a new life. His name, Carthage, associates ruin and destruction.

By the Bog of Cats is definitely a women's play; the men in it are shown to be narrow-minded, greedy and even vicious in their fact-governed decisions about how the various matters of life should be arranged. In contrast with male rationality, the desires and hopes nurtured in the souls of the female characters are accentuated by their all wearing white on the wedding day of Carthage in the drama. Between Caroline, the real bride and Hester, the discarded lover, the rivalry collapses when it turns out that the dreams of the former are not fulfilled either. Her story of once wishing for such a different ceremony also hinges on the loss of the mother:

> ... she used to take me into the bed beside her and she'd describe for me me weddin' day. Of how she'd be there with a big hat on her and so proud. And the weddin' was going to be in this big ballroom with a fountain of mermaids in the middle ... None of it was how it was meant to be, none of it. (76)

The ghost of Hester's brother, Joseph, appears to revive memories of guilt: he was killed by his own sister. Carthage witnessed the scene, and his growing alienation from the woman began with this event. A woman's guilt, like that of Hester against her brother, is never understood but severely judged in the world of patriarchal rules and laws. However, what Carthage could not see was its deeper implications: it was the act of an unfortunate, fragmented being who claims that "there's two Hester Swanes" (30), one that is conventionally decent and one that is ready to take revenge on those that deprive her of love. Joseph made her aware of the loss of her mother's feelings for her: "... I looked across the lake to my father's house and it went through me like a spear that she had a whole other life there—How could she have and I a part of her?" (74). Hester, in the wording of a critic, "embodies autochtonous Irishness—mythic, marginalised, and explosive,"[26] ambivalent and dangerous for herself as well as unwilling to move to a house in town from the bog as Carthage demands her.

---

[25] Marina Carr, *By the Bog of Cats* (Loughcrew, Oldcastle: The Gallery Press, 1999), 22. All further references are to this edition.
[26] Bruce Stewart, "'A Fatal Excess' at the Heart of Irish Atavism: review of Marina Carr's *By the Bog of Cats.*" *IASIL Newsletter* 5. 1 (1999), 1.

Unlike Hawthorne's lonely Hester who raises her child and gains recognition by serving the community, the heroine in Carr does not purport the fulfilment of moral or altruistic goals but remains interested in the self. At the end of the play she kills her own daughter to prevent her from having to relive the pain of personal history caused by the missing mother, recasting the concern with racial doom in the similarly fatal father-son scenario enacted by Yeats' *Purgatory* (1939). Hester's own death is elevated to the level of sacrifical ritual by her dance with the Ghost Fancier, suggesting spiritual transcendence while culminating in the horror of physical dismemberment by cutting out her heart to lie there "like some dark feathered bird" (81). Mother and daughter are portrayed as inseparable beings, both softly wispering "Mam—Mam—" (79, 80) as their dying words. The keenly felt lack of wholeness in the play derives from the loss of the mother and the impact of the cruel rationality of the patriarchal world, which can be understood as a powerful statement on the oppressiveness of the Oedipal narrative.[27] To paraphrase Yeats, this is no country for women.

Conclusion

Feminist theorist Hélène Cixous in her essay "Aller á la mer" reconstructs the concept of mimemis in the field of women's theatre. She contends that "If the stage is woman, it will mean ridding this space of theatricality" where "'distantiation' will not exist; on the contrary, this stage body will not hesitate to come up close, close enough to be in danger—of life."[28] These words can be applied to Carr's dramatic work as well: carefully structured on the one hand, it integrates diverse images and non-realistic modes to contest and unfix what seems certain on the surface and to probe into deeper layers. Strange, lyrical and arresting, her achievement can best be called a kind of re-familiarisation with needs and concerns haunting the Irish female sensibility on its way to fuller self-recognition.

---

[27] Cf. Jeanie Forte, op. cit. 26.
[28] Hélène Cixous, "Aller á la mer." Richard Drain (ed.), *Twentieth Century Theatre: A Sourcebook* (London: Routledge, 1995), 134.

Female Self-Cure Through Revisioning and Refashioning Male/Master Narratives in Anne Devlin's *After Easter*

Resisting Heroines

Surrounded by resurfacing social unrest and individual pain rooted in the patriarchal methods and manifestations of colonialism and its consequences, contemporary Northern Irish woman authors tend to become, to turn Judith Fetterley's phrase around, resisting writers. Focusing on female reactions, their works are necessarily informed by effects that subvert established discourses and conventional notions about the nature of Irish literature. Among the playwrights, Belfast-born Anne Devlin, in her first play for the stage, *Ourselves Alone*, has two young sisters and their sister-in-law endeavour to assert their womanly needs and individuality against the strong masculine politics of the post-colonial, Troubles-ridden background. Although they refuse to commit themselves, these protagonists cannot help experiencing that personal lives, resemblances as well as differences between people, are profoundly politicised in the Northern Ireland of the 1970-80s. The youngest of them, Frieda, develops the conviction that, in order to escape being "doubly objectified,"[1] and write her own songs in chosen subjectivity, she has to leave Ireland to find "cover" on "another part of the shore"[2] — to borrow expressions from her meaningful story at the closure of the play. The other two sisters emphasise love, emotional loyalty and motherhood as their source of personal independence. Analysed by Anthony Roche, the chief merit of the play lies in the fact that it "displays a positive deconstruction to counter the purely negative theatrics of the politicians and the bombers."[3]

In the "Author's Note" to *Ourselves Alone* Devlin, now a long-term resident in England, claims about Andersonstown, Belfast: "I used to live there — and I still do" (10), which makes it hardly a wonder that her second work for the stage, *After Easter*, leads us there again as well as to an exploration of identity. The new play dramatises the temporary homecoming and self-quest of 37 year-old Greta, a later reincarnation of Frieda laden with several more

---

[1] Ailbhe Smyth, "Paying Our Disrespects to the Bloody State We're In: Women, Violence, Culture, and the State." Joan Hoff and Maureen Coulter (eds.), *Irish Women's Voices: Past and Present*. A publication of the *Journal of Women's History* 6 (1995), 200.

[2] Anne Devlin, *Ourselves Alone* (London: Faber and Faber, 1986), 90. All further references are to this edition.

[3] Anthony Roche, *Contemporary Irish Drama from Beckett to McGuinness* (Dublin: Gill and Macmillan, 1994), 241.

stories, and reproduces, on a heightened scale, the hallucinations of the other women in *Ourselves Alone*. Beginning with Greta's account of a jumble of uncontrolled emotions and actions, screams and smiles signalling an obvious mother-daughter conflict, *After Easter* culminates in the same character's telling a beautiful, serenely coherent story to her baby about the way back to "the place where the rivers come from, where you come from..."[4] The traditional, Irish mode of oral narration at the end of Greta's journey functions as female self-articulation, situated back in the English, formerly alien context.

Greta first appears on the stage as a psychiatric patient in England following a rebellious attempt to direct attention to her distress using her body, by sitting on a road among the traffic. Her crisis proves manifold, one thread entangled with another, as being a Catholic from Ulster and living in England determines her relationships. Her ambiguous identity undermines her: during the years of her exile she has been unable to fit into the new environment, feeling multiple displacement and isolation in her mixed marriage as well as in a variety of situations: "I don't resent being Irish—I only resent it being pointed out to me" (4). The English society, as background, still accommodates racial stereotyping where, with embarrassing inconsistency, "... otherness coexists with the myth of homogeneity."[5] Greta's vulnerability both as an uprooted woman, and as one suffering from the failure of her marriage because her English husband has resented her self-explaining stories and left her emotionally, spawn ambivalent feelings in her towards her own family. Not wishing to go back to her baby but rather to her mother betrays hunger for love, the first love of life, that of the mother with whom she did not have a satisfying relationship according to the opening sentences rife with the signs of family hysteria. Greta needs to unravel the tissues of her past and finish the incomplete story between herself and her parents.

Greta's concomitant experience of sexual hypocrisy, dependence and inequality, the fact that she should not articulate her desire for extramarital liaisons openly, feeds her rage for the elimination of order, for a fundamental change in her private life: divorce. The male-centeredness of public morality is well represented by the behaviour of the hospital doctor who expects her to give clear-cut answers after his own fashion and sticks to the letter of the law made by men, emphasising the role of logic and appearances. Arguments like "Do you think in your present circumstances that any court would let you have care of children?" (4) sound both authoritative and discouraging from his mouth. Greta's personal anguish and acts of individual protest have been re-

---

[4] Anne Devlin, *After Easter* (London: Faber and Faber, 1994) 75. All further references are to this edition.

[5] Mary J. Hickman and Bronwen Walter, "Deconstructing Whiteness. Irish Women in Britain." *Feminist Review* 50 (1995), 10.

duced to "postnatal depression" (6) by her husband and the surrounding world for being different, as "madness is the lack of resemblance."[6] The problems casting their too-long shadows on her life include also the complexity of pronounced lack of faith while receiving religious messages and mystic signs. At the same time, regarding the political turmoil of her native Ulster, she is pushed to the realisation that "the difference between insanity and politics is only a matter of numbers" (3).

Allowed to leave the hospital for her parents' home at Easter, Greta carries her cross of being a mere inch away from total mental collapse burdened with real spiritual and identity confusion back to Belfast. She imagines an apparition to be her mother, screaming in a way that "felt as if the whole of Ireland was crying out to me" (11). The call of mother and mother country together set Greta on the journey to the "rag-and-bone shop of the heart" and heartland, that involves both pain and revelation for her. Greta undergoes a cure of the spirit through the stages of confrontation with her own strange impulses as well as the ghosts, tensions and embarrassments haunting both her family and environment of origin.

Sampling the reviewers' reactions to *After Easter*, one comes across largely favourable as well as mixed remarks about its composition. The critiques according to which it carries "genuine passion" but piles up far too many problems for one play,[7] and that it drags in much gratuitous material while depicting just one person's spiritual quest,[8] fail to notice that the inner picture of Greta's special female and Irish search for selfhood can barely be drawn through selected fragments. A psyche on display, the drama amasses what bubbles in its recesses with a structure fusing verbal detail with linear progress in stages rather unconventionally, but by no means "unformed," which can be heard as a commonly held charge against the writing of many women on account of their diversion from (male) mainstream efforts.[9] *After Easter* develops a challenging, integrative form, re-using, rewriting, also interrogating literary and cultural narratives/discourses in its action, images and stories, through which process a new, liberating situation emerges around the protagonist. The intertexts incorporated by the play in a pattern of imbrication assume alternative vistas as well as changed endings, striving to voice stories

---

[6] Shoshana Felman, "Women and Madness: the Critical Fallacy." Catherine Belsey and Jane Moore (eds.), *The Feminist Reader: Essays in Gender and the Politics of Literary Criticism* (London: Macmillan, 1989), 147.

[7] Nick. Curtis, Review of *After Easter*. *Theatre Record* (26 May - 8 April 1995), 399.

[8] Alastair Macaulay, Review of *After Easter*. *Theatre Record* (21 May - 3 June 1994), 699.

[9] Meany, Helen. "The State of Play." *Theatre Ireland* 30 (1993), 33.

"that would turn out differently" according to Nancy Miller[10] and not merely echo or reinforce the male-inscribed traditions and practices of both literature and life. The present paper aims to inquire into the textual realisation of Greta's journey, analysing its self-healingly provocative dialogue with a range of literary, mythical and cultural materials created and used by male authors or sanctified by patriarchal societies.

Religion and Selfhood

Coincidentally, August Strindberg's morality play, *Easter* (1901) was revived in London shortly before the staging of Devlin's new work.[11] Set in a "terrible town, where everyone hates everyone else,"[12] not unlike war-time Belfast, its action follows the homecoming of Eleonora from mental hospital at Easter time, while the father is interned, working towards a reconciliation in the family and freedom from the threat of total financial ruin. After much melancholy and pain, Strindberg's family finally enjoy peace and grace, with Eleonora happily planning a trip to the country and the curtain falls on her brother and his fiancée approaching each other in rekindled love. Running counter to the several features shared with *Easter*, *After Easter* refuses to perpetuate the conventions of the dramatic narrative in Strindberg's way, avoiding "a reinscription of the dominant order" by restoring a previous, supposedly happy status quo to fulfill the demand of the patriarchal system for stability in the family that classic realism involves.[13] Devlin's Greta leaves again, having reached an altered perception of herself and others by the end of the play.

Strindberg's Easter-time story is imbued with incidents and details that associate Eleonora as well as some other characters with Christ and his Passion. The girl speaks of herself as "dead" (135) and later adds "... it's Easter, and we must suffer" (141). Analysing the figure of Eleonora for the actress who was to incarnate her on stage for the first time, Strindberg claimed that "... she shares the suffering of every living creature, or, to put it another way, realizes the idea of 'Christ in Man'"[14] Elis, the brother, complains of

---

[10] Qtd. in Gisela Ecker, "'A Map for Re-reading': Intertextualität aus der Perspektive einer feministischen Literaturwissenschaft." Ulrich Broich und Manfred Pfister (eds.), *Intertextualität* (Tübingen: Max Niemeyer, 1985), 307.
[11] Anne Devlin claims not to have known Strindberg's play before composing her own.
[12] August Strindberg, *Easter. Three Plays*. Trans. Peter Watts. (London: Penguin Books, 1958), 125. All further references are to this edition.
[13] Jeanie Forte, "Realism, Narrative, and the Feminist Playwright—a Problem of Reception." Helene Keyssar (ed.), *Feminist Theatre and Theory* (London: Macmillan, 1996), 20-21.
[14] Qtd. in Olof Lagercrantz, *August Strindberg*. Trans. Anselm Hollo. (London: Faber and Faber, 1979), 301.

impending betrayal by one of his students, who bears the name of Peter, the disciple denying Jesus publicly. The documents about their father's legal trial and confession with "the tape and the red seals" make him think of "the five wounds of Jesus" (147). Christ's words on the cross find an echo in the mother's anguished outcry: "My God, why hast thou forsaken me—and my children?" (152). Having been visited by the devil, Greta in *After Easter* also embodies Christ-like features: human betrayal and suffering of inhuman proportions befall her. In a remarkably vivid account of one of her numerous visions she describes the experience of dying in loneliness, face-to-face with the universe:

> GRETA   … I was lying out under the stars with the night wind on my face and I was so close to the heavens, as if I were lying on top of a mountain, that I could see quite clearly the star constellation. I was in such despair that I opened my mouth and let out a huge cry until my voice filled the whole sky. And I felt it leave my body and go up into the stars. I did. And I knew I had died that night. (14)

Transforming the signs born by the haunting voices and hallucinations, she also seems to be moving towards some sacred goal: "Now all I have to do is wait — …To see what I am being prepared for" (17-18). From torment and psychic death the parallel of the story of Easter promises resurrection, and this happens in both Strindberg's and Devlin's plays. Eleonora trusts that they will be saved, but remains passive; it is Lindkvist, the businessman who functions as a deus ex machina, his "corrective figure"[15] re-establishing order and happiness by the magic touch of deciding not to require the family to pay him his due. In contrast, Devlin allows the female protagonist, Greta, to arrive at resurrection through her own personal development, informed by a spiritual quest for understanding, as she puts it into the beautifully enigmatic words: "I did so want to be full of light" (20).

Greta's Easter narrative concludes with a hard-earned story that deploys flying astride a stag higher and higher as "a redemptive pre-Christian symbol."[16] Combining the female and the pagan, strengthened by the etymological derivation of "Easter" from the name of an ancient dawn-goddess, eastre, Devlin's play negotiates a more inclusive version to the male-centered Christian symbolism of the festival, while radically differing from Strindberg. At the same time, it invites comparison with other texts where Easter and personal renewal are linked, for instance Laurie Lee's poem "The Easter Green" that

---

[15] Birgitta Steene, *The Greatest Fire. A Study of A. Strindberg* (Carbondale and Edwardsville: Southern Illinois Univ. Press, 1973), 94.
[16] Anne Devlin, *Letter to the Author,* 5 October 1995.

depicts the "prodigal" anointed by "the green blood flushing at the heart"[17] against a setting of both religion and lush nature pictured through the male lens. In the field of drama the male, as well as the Protestant approach of Stewart Parker, another Belfast-born writer who spent years away from his hometown (in the USA), may well have meant a natural challenge for a female protester like Anne Devlin. Because of the parallel of Easter and Pentecost, and both plays dealing with the ghosts of the past and the misunderstandings of the present in Belfast, Devlin's *After Easter* most resembles Stewart Parker's *Pentecost* (1987) in contemporary Irish drama. However, their endings prise open differences in both strategy and outlook: Parker's characters quote mainly the Bible while Devlin's Greta forges her own pre-Christian story to celebrate reconciliation, in which her solution is "bodied forth," not explained.[18]

Endowed with second sight, Strindberg's Eleonora is a character close to religious mysticism, though the text contains a slight indication that the drugs she had to take in hospital were partly responsible for this quality. *After Easter* expands the social theme by constructing a subversive approach to certain aspects and manifestations of the Catholic Church and religion from its angle of female resignification. With the seemingly crazy ideas that "everyone is the Virgin Mary" (2) and "I am a Catholic, a Protestant, a Hindu, a Moslem, a Jew" (7) Greta suggests deposition of the male deity from supremacy and refuses monolithic religiousness. Then, as part of her personal story she mentions a Catholic school in England where she found herself exposed to insults like "They used to call me the Irish Art Teacher. And the girls used to say in front of me—as if to offend me—as if I cared: Father So and So's a bog Irish priest" (13). Weakening still further her already crumbling self confidence, this must have been rooted in the long tradition of maintaining national inferiority feelings in the Irish even with the help of Catholicism in England.[19] To interpret the disturbing gap between her lack of faith and hallucinations connected with religion Greta, exactly on Good Friday in the narrative sequence of the drama (scene 3), visits Elish, her cousin in a Belfast convent where she lives as prioress. Her convent name, Bethany, coincides with that of the place where Jesus stayed in the house of Simon the leper, and received ointment on his head poured from an alabaster flask by a woman, thus preparing him for

---

[17] Laurie Lee, "The Easter Green." Phyllis M. Jones (ed.), *Modern Verse 1900-1950* (London: Oxford Univ. Press, 1965), 246-47.

[18] Judith Thompson, "'The World Made Flesh': Women and Theatre." Adrian Page (ed.), *The Death of the Playwright: Modern British Drama and Literary Theory* (London: Macmillan, 1992), 34.

[19] Cf. Mary J. Hickman and Bronwen Walter, op. cit. 11.

burial as Jesus explained to the indignant disciples. With this element, the notion of discrepancy between acts, intentions and interpretations is introduced.

In her psychic despair, Greta hopes to unravel the meaning of her mystical experiences aided by Elish-Bethany, a representative of the faith. The confession-like story of her Pentecostal visions of flame and rebirth by liberating herself of the evil spirit, however, elicits a truly unexpected response. The nun shares her own story with Greta about an unhappy childhood, her almost inevitable joining the order and the lack of grace in spite of all her immersion in religious practices and high position. Stymied and agonised she bursts into tears and even baffling accusations at the end, which prove revelatory also with regard to the Church. The officially declared healing power of convent-life, where personal woes can and have to be forgotten about are diametrically contradicted. Elish gives vent to so far suppressed feelings in the presence of Greta, normally silenced by the general assumptions and internalised rules of the Church. A tension of this nature could be alleviated only through the kind of change that a recent feminist study envisions: "We need to hear the voices of women religious, the self which is no longer chronicler but the subject of the testimony."[20] But under its modernised surface, where nuns no longer have to wear a veil at all times, the convent has remained the stronghold of patriarchal dogmas, with only the priests considered empowered. Greta rejects the recuperated Elish's suggestion that she should reconcile herself to the demands of the Catholic Church to find protection and use her "spiritual gift" within its bonds. Bending to these, she realises, could in no way enable her to undertake her real self and live in the "main room" (28) of her life instead of the "outer room" (26) where a troubled national and domestic situation as well as her husband's rejection of her stories together with herself have exiled her.

Eleonora's story in Strindberg becomes complicated by her compulsion to enter a shop and snatch a daffodil, the Swedish name of which translates into English as "Easter lily."[21] Although she leaves there a krona for the flower, the news of theft spreads, the paper takes it up and the police are alerted. The ambiguity of her thoughtless action dissolves only after a time, the story itself resembling in miniature her father's financial entanglements, pointing also to mercy, good intentions not endlessly misperceived. In *After Easter*, under the weight of the political situation troubling Belfast, Greta engages in an act of iconoclasm: she steals a chalice to distribute wafers to people all over the town "to stop the killings" (50) while criticising the "hypocrisy of the churches in Ireland to condemn violence and to keep the schools apart" (49). Obeying her "Voices" like Saint Joan, she also earns the misrepresentation of the official

---

[20] Margaret MacCurtain, "Late in the Field: Catholic Sisters in Twentieth-Century Ireland and the New Religious History." Joan Hoff and Maureen Coulter (eds.), op. cit. 58.
[21] Olof Lagercrantz, op. cit. 299.

voices of the patriarchal society, the Northern Irish press having written about her protest according to its purposes: "... they decide what it means. Because they don't listen. And they don't look" (58). Speaking to herself here marks Greta's inner, self-healing transformation through the recognition of how the insanity of the circumstances, where one-sided interpretations dominate, prevents people from expressing their own meanings. With this conspicuous broadening of thematic embedding, the treatment of the stolen religious object in Devlin's play effects greater complexity than what is achieved by Strindberg's use of the motif. Greta also rises to the level of connecting the individual wish to bring peace to people outside the church with a larger, pressing objective, that of real human equality: "If a woman can be a priest, God can be female.... It means that women might be loved" (57).

Female Bonding Versus Bending

In *Easter* the untying of knots shifts into male hands: the family is saved by Lindkvist's forgiveness and charity returning Eleonora's father's one-time kindness to him, which he relates in a decisive conversation with Elis. Greta's redemption in *After Easter*, signalled by her wish to go home to her children in a state of enriched spiritual awareness and understanding, works out chiefly through the bonding of women that emerges in the play, refocusing its predecessor's frames of reference. The female pattern set by *Ourselves Alone* resurfaces in *After Easter* with Greta accompanied by her younger sisters, Aoife and Helen who, at first sight, seem to represent diverging attitudes to their Irishness and gender. Through her name Aoife relates to Celtic legend, reinforcing the inevitability of her home-made, artless, protective nationalism, tellingly showing itself when, to ease Greta's marriage troubles, she proclaims the easy solution: "Say what you like — but this I believe, the English and the Irish cannot love each other" (7). Then, to explain Greta's recounted nocturnal vision of stars, connected with her "death," Aoife exclaims: "The Plough! You saw the symbol of the Irish Citizen Army!" (15). The unmarried Helen, a commercial artist who leads the life of an ambitious top girl in London, insists that Greta could have seen the Pleiades, the seven stars, considered to be a cluster of female images. Sighting stars is also a motif in Strindberg: the protagonist of *Easter* mentions her daylight contemplating Cassiopeia, a W-shaped constellation in the Milky Way. However, beyond stressing the idea of Eleonora's being special, no more meaning derives from the briefly mentioned experience. In *After Easter*, both the sign and its interpretations open the text up to viewing the individual woman's predicament from the widened perspective of intersecting discourses, enshrined best in Hélène Cixous's words: "In woman, personal history blends together with the history of all women, as well as national and world history."[22]

In Homer's world, Helen embodies a beauty dangerous for men without much elaboration of the fact that, having been carried to Troy, she lives in imposed exile. Devlin's Helen deliberately plays down her Irishness by imitating an American accent behind which deceptive cosmopolitanism self-protection lurks: to eschew identification as Irish and, therefore, being regarded with suspicion in Britain. The parallel between the Greek and Irish Helens unfolds not only in the names, but concerning also their new homes, since London has been identified with imperial Rome and even with Troy, from where the Romans originated. Through the orchestration of the implications of Helen's exiled fate, culminating in the determination to make a major change, Devlin joins those writers who point towards the possible renegotiation of female inscription in one of the founding myths of European culture.[23] On the other hand, attributing "street currency to a high cultural literary trope,"[24] another aspect of the motif presents itself when Manus, the women's brother, responds to being called "Paddy" and "a thicko micko" by patrolling British soldiers in a series of insults, ending with "Down with Troy!" (53). The text provides further examples of dismantling conventional cognitive and linguistic structures to articulate the reactions of the people who live in troubled, sectarian Belfast, where the IRA men can be "our ones" as well as "murdering bastards" (42) for members of the same family, here the mother and Helen. Above all divisions human suffering evokes compassion, as Aoife understandingly depicts it, beginning with "us" and arriving at the consideration of "them": "It must be hard to be an English soldier" (55). Greta herself inserts the double paradox of "We have the faith of the killers and the guilt of the spared" (56). "You can stay and get away" (70) runs Manus's remark about the possibility of re-appropriating individual liberation from the impact of sectarian strife.

Aoife arrives on stage early in the drama with a fractured wrist due to a quarrel with her husband which infuriated her to chase him with the carpet cleaner, a highly comic echo of legendary woman-warrior Aoife's ability to fight, whom even Cuchulain could defeat only by means of a trick. Devlin's Aoife, comparably to some other female characters in modern Irish drama from Winnie in Beckett's *Happy Days* to Lily in Friel's *The Freedom of the*

---

22 Hélene Cixous, "The Laugh of the Medusa." Elaine Marks and I. de Courtivron (eds.), *New French Feminisms*. Trans. Keith Cohen and Paula Cohen (Brighton: Harvester, 1980), 252-53.

23 Claire Buck, "'O Careless, Unspeakable Mother': Irigaray, H. D. and Maternal Origin." Susan Sellers (ed.), *Feminist Criticism: Theory and Practice* (New York: Harvester, 1991), 133.

24 Elizabeth Butler Cullingford, "British Romans and Irish Carthaginians: Anticolonial Metaphor in Heaney, Friel, and McGuinness." *PMLA* 111.2. (1996), 236.

City, resorts to humour to combat her frustration over not having married the man she would have liked and her failure to seduce other men. When in scene 6 the family crouch under the table to protect themselves from what seems brewing outside, she recollects her funny poem entitled "Corpuscles of Love," written about a kiss (70). Through corpuscles that refer to both the red and white cells of the blood, the meaning of love expands towards harmony between opposites and then and there Aoife becomes reconciled to her marriage, like Molly Bloom at the end of *Ulysses.* After all, only Daimon, her husband thought the poem wonderful and gave Aoife the prize of a kiss for it.

As the play progresses, more and more is conjured up from behind the mask of differences coded in the often hilarious remarks and clichés, with which the sisters cover their personal wounds, thus highlighting the intersection of inner worlds. All of them have to come to terms with emotional problems, the effect of failed/failing relationships, and together they form a kind of collective subject.[25] Their raising, and frank discussion of, a range of sexual, marital and psychic problems from within the frame of female experience in a language free of constraints effectively opposes the discursive exclusion that women often face in the communal ethics of modern societies. Complementary to Greta's marriage pushed to the brink of divorce, Helen's current affair involves a lover whose "wife is younger, prettier, but he comes to talk to me" (19). However, she does not answer his phone call when her sisters are in the flat and Greta's case needs to be discussed. In a comic summary of her extramarital flirtations Aoife subverts the traditional Irish connection between religious faith and sexual morality: "I just say, 'I know I'm married to you, God, but would you mind if I had a wee fling with So and So?' ... If it happens, it (the answer) was yes. If it doesn't, it was no" (68).

On visiting their sick father in hospital the sisters meet Emer, a country girl who has moved to Belfast to become a nurse, whose situation recalls the mythological Emer's as well as Greta's own: her husband abandoned her for a more powerful woman. It is Greta who comes forward with the clue that women without the necessary "bite" and "something crucial ... aligned" (41) to their disposition are likely to suffer erasure from moulding the course of their lives. In the same hospital they see a pregnant woman, Melda, diagnosed mad, who proves to be a kind of foil for Greta. Her babies were taken away from her because of her psychic condition, yet she dances to the music Manus plays and this "dream language ... suggests a different way of responding to experi-

---

[25] Cf. Sue-Ellen Case, "From Split Subject to Split Britches." Enoch Brater (ed.), *Feminine Focus: The New Women Playwrights* (Oxford: Oxford Univ. Press, 1989), 143.

ence, a dance of alternative possibilities which offers, ... a potential escape route from a fixity of response."[26]

The increasingly emphasised closeness of the three women, exposing the vulnerability of Aoife and Helen in spite of their more pronounced personal security, enlivens the play with shared humanity, itself an ancient source of healing. Having "more flexible, less rigid ego boundaries than men" and managing to "define themselves through relationships,"[27] these female characters work out miracles among themselves. As early as scene 2, Aoife voices the agenda of psychic cure for Greta: "She needs to find herself first" (9). At the end of the play, Greta and Helen, the two exiles on their return to England, find the means to assist each other in re-constructing their identities. The former almost commits suicide when she stands on the top of Westminster Bridge clutching in a bag the ashes of the beloved father, a symbol of her whole past. It is Helen who deters her from the deed, back to wishing to live and to go home: "—let him go! Don't rot the lives of your children on his account!" (73). Helen gains power over Greta as she herself undergoes a change through her unashamed self-scrutiny and by acknowledging that she did have a role in Greta's loss of balance: "I'm your opposite and I won't let you change into what it is you want to become. You want to be an artist and I won't let you because I'm the artist in the family. You want to be a beautiful woman and I won't let you because I've always been the beautiful woman in the family" (72).

By their names Greta and Helen evoke the two female characters destined to be emotional satellites moving round the hero in Goethe's *Faust*. In contrast, Devlin recasts her women as independent individuals, as subjects not objects. Gretchen in *Faust* undergoes personal hell through disturbed motherhood and dislodgement, condemned by Satan but finally redeemed by God. Devlin's Greta enacts personal redemption, hearing not a voice from above like Gretchen but that of a baby laughing in her ear, guiding her home, to the power of motherhood. Helen in *After Easter* appears as a kind of female Faust when criticising herself on a more explicitly philosophical plane as well: "...the worst thing I did was to squander a great gift. I took my gift, which was very powerful and I used that power to seduce and dominate. When I should have used that power to create and free" (73). Finally, emphasising the influence of Greta on herself, Helen describes her own experience, paralleling that of her sister's: she has had to feel pain to glimpse a vision of "wings and

[26] Geraldine Cousin, *Women in Dramatic Place and Time: Contemporary Female Characters on Stage* (Routledge: London and New York, 1996), 195.
[27] Judith Kegan Gardiner, "Mind Mother: Psychoanalysis and Feminism." Gayle Greene and Coppélia Kahn (eds.), *Making a Difference: Feminist Literary Criticism* (London: Methuen, 1985), 135.

eyes of light" (74). The light then disappears from her daily life but remains hidden inside the soul forever, like Ireland herself, to be carried wherever she goes. Human transformation strengthened by mutuality urges Helen to realise that she has to forget to be able to see, and Greta to hear the call of her child. The magical place of both Helen's and Greta's is one in the soul, the centre of inner peace and freedom, indicating the real homecoming to the self, which does not depend on specific location because it is not determined by outside sources.

The Law of the Mother and Finding Personal Language

The final victory of Greta over the law of the father, the paralysing chains of the patriarchal system, results from not only revisiting her parents but also re-viewing the complex effect of their relationship on the formation of their children's identity, a theme not explored in Strindberg's *Easter*. Her brother, Manus, plays here a key-role; the fact that he and Greta have been their father's favourites makes it more difficult for them to come to terms with their inheritance, the parental influence having been contradictory between two extremes as it was. Manus's reported oscillation between hetero- and homo-sexuality suggests an incomplete boy-father identification. By playing an Irish tune on his fiddle at the Belfast hospital, meeting with a predictably mixed reception, he expresses the need to counterbalance the father's anti-nationalism (due to his Marxist belief), which did not let them study "the music, the language, the culture" (39) of their own people. On the other hand, the mother, Rose, a dealer in first communion veils, is said to have "made up for it" (39). Scene 6 stages the wake at the body of the dead father and, characteristically for the Irish tradition, the corpse is not only physically present but listens and talks, in this case to Greta, who now sees clearly about her state of exile. She complains of being "a copier … out of fear" like many other rootless people whose clock does not work in the new home, England, where she hears from their speech that "there are no individuals, only scattered phrases and competing ideas" (59). The story told about her fellow-immigrants reifies her own fundamental identity problem in the masculine society of the other island.

Before this point in the narrative of Devlin's work, the conflict between the father and the mother has already been hinted at in several forms, most poignantly through Greta's stories about Rose's jealousy of her husband's love of their oldest daughter. Entrenched in the protagonist's memory there is the one-time recognition of the power of books, connected with the kindling of family tension: "… there was a book she'd been reading that summer—a cheap pornographic story of incest, the rape of a girl by her father. When mother read this story it drove her mad. She used to run in screaming: 'Where is he? Where are you hiding him?'" (20). Structured around the wake there follows further probing into the real nature of parental influences. The children first identify themselves with the dead father, the loss of whom seems to disorder family life and makes them relive its painful contradictions. However, out of the chaos of hurts and accusations there evolves a commonly achieved reconciliation and deeper awareness of both parents' values and shortcomings, remodelling the extremes conceptualised on the axis of the Oedipal complex and destabilising the Freudian scenario. The mother is allowed to explain herself in defence against her children's misinterpretation of her ambitions, deeds and weaknesses. Myths about the patriarchal configuration of fixed role assignments are questioned with the disclosure that Michael, the father, could afford to live for his ideas but Rose has had to do business and count pennies to make ends meet. Very importantly, Greta herself acquires leadership in revalorising the mother's role in the family, at last capable of understanding the roots of the latter's hysteria as the corollary of lacking the kindness she craved for in her marriage. Her identification with the devalued mother suffering from a confused self-esteem has been a difficult process for Greta, like for many other women in modern societies according to Nancy Chodorow's analysis of the frequent rejection of Oedipal maternal identification and its implications.[28]

Greta even reunites the parents in the love they must have had for each other under the surface of daily conflicts by referring to the father's account of a dream: "… it was raining…your mother and I used to fish in the rain … she was a better fisherman than I was" (62). The symbolism of fish and fisherman evokes the Christian idea of love and peace, and with her caring behaviour Greta finally manages to make peace between her mother and her sisters too, the object of quarrel being the father's fishing sweater which then goes from one to the other as a token of reconsolidated bonding and reconfirmed love. The family scene is seasoned with liberating humour that derives from playful gender confusion in revealing and thus comprehending the interrelation of the national and personal levels of feminised, weakened, copied existence:

GRETA   But why did she beat us and not the others?
HELEN   Because you said everything he felt.
AOIFE   It wasn't that. It was because you two looked more like my
        daddy. She used to call him Kate. Then she'd say (*Pointing* to
        GRETA) DupliKate and TripliKate (*Pointing to* MANUS). (67)

The family reunion ends in looking for safety together in the war-time circumstances and, tragicomically, with a mocking touch of O'Casey in it, the

---

[28] Nancy Chodorow, *Feminism and Psychoanalytic Theory* (New Haven: Yale Univ. Press, 1989), 64.

mother celebrates their diving under the table with the corpse on top saying: "This is nice, isn't it. We're all together again" (70).

Back in London, scattering their father's ashes from the top of Westminster Bridge to let them carried away by the wind into the water, Greta stresses the symbolic end to the past by reciting lines from Wordsworth's *Composed Upon Westminster Bridge, September 3, 1802*. She mixes in her own tormented observations, disrupting the original romantic picture that "takes civilization back into nature with a pantheistic embrace."[29] A version of the first line of the Wordsworthian poem is quoted in Stewart Parker's *Spokesong* as well, by Frank, though only to endorse his idealism about using bicycles to save time and peace in the modern world. In Devlin altered lines like "Dull would he be of soul who could pass by a sight so touching—as the homeless on Westminster Bridge" (71) imply the immigrant situation, but at the end of Greta's quote homecoming for the Irish in London seems to unfold: "Silent bare—ships, towers, domes, theatres and temples lie open unto the Irish" (71).

In *Easter* the reconciliation between mother and daughter stems from the former's realisation that her child is both good and sane, and finds a highly conventional expression, sealed by a kiss: "My child—my darling child. You have come back to me, and you shall stay with me" (165). The ending of the play itself involves fairy-tale-like elements and the image of the child used in a wider sense. Lindkvist names himself as "the Giant from Skinnarviksberg" (173) who has come to rearrange all and "make the children good" (174). Eleonora bids him farewell in a like manner: "Thank you, nice Giant" (174). The concluding story of Greta's in *After Easter* about coming "to the place" (75) after Easter is told to her baby about her mother and origin, restoring the significance of the mother-daughter relationship, downgraded in Freudian psychology, but itself a "great unwritten story" worth retelling in the opinion of Adrienne Rich.[30] Set in nature and harmony amidst changes, describing escape from the cold and fear, Greta's story does not attribute omnipotence to the mother but poetically encodes the possibility of feeling the mother to be the daughter as well, a unique reciprocity outlined by Luce Irigaray.[31] At the same time, the symbol of the stag places Greta beside Peer Gynt, Ibsen's hero whose story about his world-viewing adventures riding a stag up to the moun-

---

[29] Péter Egri, *Value and Form: Comparative Literature, Painting and Music* (Budapest: Tankönyvkiadó, 1993), 74.
[30] Adrienne Rich, *Of Woman Born: Motherhood as Experience and Institution* (London: Virago Press Ltd., 1977), 225.
[31] Margaret Whitford, (ed.), *The Irigaray Reader* (Cambridge Mass.: Basil Blackwell, 1991), 50.

tains is set at the beginning of the well-known play. This way Greta re-appropriates women's potential in reaching out to the vital meanings of human life:

> GRETA   ... My mother and I were hunting. But because of the cold we couldn't feel anything or find anything to eat. So we sat down by the stream. I looked up and saw it suddenly, a stag, antlered and black, profiled against the sky.... My mother was afraid, but I saw it was only hungry. I took some berries from my bag and fed the stag from the palm of my hand. The stag's face was frozen and I had to be careful because it wanted to kiss me, and if I had let it, I would have died of cold. But gradually as it ate, its face was transformed and it began to take on human features. And then the thaw set in—I could hear the stream running, and the snow began to melt. I could hear all the waters of the forest rushing and it filled my ears with a tremendous sound. *(Pause.)* So I got on the stag's back and flew with it to the top of the world. (75)

After so many puzzled and even painful stories of Greta and the other characters, the play closes when she finally adds: "and this is my own story" (75). The cycle of the protagonist's search for her own song in *Ourselves Alone* comes full circle here, voicing a self-invented resolution to relocate her in the chainless world of love and the personal, revitalising her art at the same time. Though Greta counts as one of the "dinosaurs" she refers to (71), a race "lost in the old society," as the Irish derisively cast those Irish who live in Britain,[32] she has certainly grown to be a specimen to question this designation. Her final story also suggests a new beginning, defying the 'beginning—middle—end' kind of narratives which, according to Edward Said, relate to paternity and hierarchy,[33] to masculine (and colonial) master narratives. Its focus on maternity valorises the pre-Oedipal state beyond the patriarchal, which does not yet know differences.

Conclusion: Confronting Traditions from Within

Joyce, the indisputable patriarch of modern Irish literature, can be discerned as a golden thread throughout Devlin's drama. Greta displays some resemblance to her namesake in *The Dead* on account of her strong concern with the past, her deep-rooted Irishness and her self-articulating storytelling. But she goes further than Joyce's heroine in subverting the patriarchal and finding her

---

[32] Clara Connolly et al., "Editorial to the Irish Issue: The British Question." *Feminist Review* 50 (1995), 3.
[33] Qtd. in Toril Moi, *Sexual/Textual Politics: Feminist Literary Theory* (London and New York: Methuen, 1985), 68.

own way. On the other hand, her visions of the devil recall Stephen Dedalus's torment at the memory of the so deeply implanted force of questioned/abandoned Catholicism. However, Greta's remorseful unease about religion becomes dispelled when, to the ghost of her father, she at last sums up how she had been expelled from the once attended Dominican school following disagreement with a nun: "She said, 'You're not the sort of girl we want in this school.' So I tried to pull off her veil" (60). Anger is shown at the root of misbehaviour with the Dominican, the welling up of inner protest, the opposite of willingness to suppress, acted out in the teeth of the obligation to conform. Joyce's *Exiles* also incarnates a dramatic parallel for Devlin because of deploying the theme of return from exile, an intriguing one in Irish literature that enables the writers to confront their main character(s) with the past and the milieu shaping their present and influencing their future. Greta's voices, however, do not tell her to despair, as happens to Richard Rowan while strolling on the revisited island. Her self-searching ends in self-celebration, her story emphasising both recurrence and continuity, adding also to Strindberg's Nitzschean conclusion about not only the bad but the good coming back.

As a primarily inner drama of quest, its texture and style rendering "discernible the indiscernible,"[34] *After Easter* elaborates both the need for and the possibility of rebirth through suffering and self-confrontation, orchestrated through dialogue with the ongoing narratives of the patriarchal culture. Meanwhile it remains pronouncedly Irish, reformulating as its guiding creed the nowadays not always welcome Yeatsian notion, put into the musician's, Manus's mouth: "All great art will have the tribe behind it" (39). With the female and the national so effectively but untraditionally bonded, Devlin contributes as artist to expanding "the horizons of Irish sexual and national identity."[35] Not less importantly, by weaving the serious with the comic, *After Easter* plays on a great variety of tone and its dense linguistic richness links it to the best work written for the Irish stage.

---

[34] Carole Woddis, Review of *After Easter. Theatre Record* (21 May - 3 June 1994), 699.
[35] Gerardine Meaney, *Sex and Nation: Women in Irish Culture and Politics* (Dublin: Attic Press, 1991), 18.

New Strangers in the House? Immigrants and Natives in Donal O'Kelly's *Asylum! Asylum!* and John Barrett's *Borrowed Robes*

Exile and Asylum

As substantially documented in the social histories written about the country, emigration, exile and return to a transformed homeland have become part of the Irish national experience, forming a tradition remarkable for its "longevity and intensity."[1] In the domain of modern Irish literature hundreds of works are known that address the economic, communal as well as spiritual aspects of living elsewhere, with special regard to their profound effects on identity and self-awareness. After notable antecedents deploying the theme in its many-sidedness, the second revival of Irish drama, unfolding by the early 1960s, turned to Ireland's immediate social realities with an ever so great eagerness and, in Fintan O'Toole's words, was "almost entirely driven by an attempt to get to grips with emigration."[2] Different as they are, John B. Keane's *Many Young Men of Twenty* (1961), Thomas Murphy's *A Whistle in the Dark* (1961), *A Crucial Week in the Life of a Grocer's Assistant* (1969) and *Conversations on a Homecoming* (1985) all revolve around the complexities of emigration in the context of postcolonial Ireland. However, it is in the work of Brian Friel, from *The Enemy Within* (1962) to *Molly Sweeney* (1994) through *Philadelphia, Here I Come!*, *The Loves of Cass McGuire* (1966) and *Faith Healer* (1979), that the richest use of the topos can be encountered. Intertwining the psychic and cultural aspects of exile and/or return from it with the dichotomy between the public and the private, the plays dramatize the universal burden of "the tragic distance subsisting between consciousness (informed by memory) and experience (or history)."[3]

According to Jim Mac Laughlin, Ireland's recent emigration has been characterized by many "as 'new wave emigration,' a 'European phenomenon,' and a 'new departure,'" acknowledging, at the same time, the tendency "to treat emigrants as enterprising individuals, rather than seeing them as social

---

[1] Michael D. Higgins, Declan Kiberd, "Culture and Exile: The Global Irish." *New Hibernia Review* 1. 3 (1997), 11.
[2] Fintan O'Toole, "The Ex-Isle of Erin: Emigration and Irish Culture." Jim Mac Laughlin (ed.), *Location and Dislocation in Contemporary Irish Society: Emigration and Irish Identities* (Cork: Cork Univ. Press, 1997), 168.
[3] Christopher Murray, *Twentieth-century Irish drama: mirror up to nation* (Manchester: Manchester Univ. Press, 1997) 168.

class victims."[4] Set against this change, the 1990s have been witnessing the appearance of the issue of multinationalism on the Irish stage, among others in works that deal with the question of how newcomers are treated and tolerated by the native population. Emigration from Ireland is thus contrasted as well as complicated by its opposite, the emerging problem of immigration to Ireland. What renders this theme timely is the fact that the economic prosperity of the Republic tends to attract a rapidly growing number of people from developing countries seeking asylum. The situation demanded the passing of a new law to replace the by our time totally inadequate 1935 act regarding aliens in the country. Yet the Refugee Act drafted in 1996 did not become ratified, leaving Ireland without a clearly defined immigration policy.[5] On the other hand, the issue of immigration to Ireland can be observed from the perspective of the phenomenon of globalization itself, a characteristic of our age that Edward Said describes in his "Reflections on Exile" as one of "modern warfare, imperialism and quasi-theological ambitions of totalitarian rulers ... the age of the refugee, the displaced person, mass immigration."[6]

In contemporary Irish society certain psychological patterns recognizably linked with the colonial heritage are still identified, including "lack of pride, mistrust, and devisiveness ... a narrow identity or definition of being Irish, lack of assertiveness and a tendency to oppress others."[7] Though far from being obvious in day-to-day interaction, these might become activated under the stress of some unusual incident or development. The fragility of tolerance toward otherness and perceiving the implications of multiculturalism with anguish have their roots in the historical past, when the arrival of strangers often proved to be an intrusion carrying real or potential danger for the indigenous population. In this context, among the Irish themselves, there is a great deal of disagreement and controversy regarding the subject of mass immigration and asylum-seeking. Public debates about such questions tend to encompass, indirectly as the case may be, the most sensitive points of the national consciousness. The global inevitably impacting the local, the "process of integration in a

[4] Jim Mac Laughlin, "The New Vanishing Irish: Social Characteristics of the 'New Wave' Irish Emigration." Jim Mac Laughlin (ed.), op. cit. 135, 143.
[5] Catherine Piola, "Irlande, terre d'exile/terre d'asile?" *Cycnos: Irlande-Exils* 15. 2 (1998), 61-65.
[6] Qtd. in Una Chaudhuri, *Staging Place: The Geography of Modern Drama* (Ann Arbor: The Univ. of Michigan Press, 1997), 14.
[7] Geraldine Moane, "A psychological analysis of colonialism in an Irish context." *The Irish Journal of Psychology* 15. 2, 3 (1994), 259.

multinational and multicultural Europe has created fears of a loss of identity" and "generated a new type of xenophobia" in Ireland.[8]

The Foreign Other and His Doubles

There seems to be a dialectical relationship between the variety of attitudes to the dislocation of the foreign other and the nature of the problems it brings to the surface in the host community. The present paper investigates the recent dramatic portrayal of the fate of immigrants in Irish society, as it challenges the self-images, personal ambitions and social mores of the natives. The two plays under scrutiny are both constructed around real events, which they fictionalize as artistic material. Donal O'Kelly's *Asylum! Asylum!* of 1994 reaches back to the 1991 Bucoro incident in Northern Uganda, reported in Amnesty International, whereas John Barrett's *Borrowed Robes* (1998) reflects on the Limerick pogrom against local Jews in 1904. Granting that these events were wide apart historically as well as geographically, yet one finds that in both plays the main subject incorporates the ambivalent attitudes of Irish protagonists as members of a community riven by its own problematical identification processes. "The contemporaneity of the national present," writes Homi K. Bhabha, "is always disturbed by another temporality" in a postcolonial society,[9] which underpins O'Kelly's and Barrett's works by the recent event evoking the traumas of the past and the distant event evoking present social and cultural tensions.

O'Kelly, the author of *Asylum! Asylum!*, "is a political activist, a cofounder of Calypso, a Glasgow-Dublin production company specializing in dramas dealing with human rights issues."[10] The central character of the present play of his is an intelligent young man, Joseph, who craves to obtain refugee status in Ireland since in his home country, Uganda, soldiers tortured him and burned his father alive in his presence for the supposed crime of hiding rebel arms. The violent story he presents is written on his body too, in the form of scars and bruises. By the beginning of the drama, Joseph's case has reached a turning point: he resisted deportation by jumping off the plane that was to carry him back to Uganda, and now he needs legal assistance to submit an appeal for asylum. His plight is dramatized in the context of an Irish family, the Gaughrans, whose members are, in respective ways, joined to official

---

[8] Heiner Zimmermann, "European Xenophobia and Ireland. A Postcolonial View: Donal O'Kelly: *Asylum! Asylum!*" Bernhard Reitz (ed.), *Race and Religion in Contemporary Theatre and Drama in English* (Trier: Wissenschaftlicher Verlag, 1999), 67.

[9] Homi K. Bhabha, *The Location of Culture* (London: Routledge, 1994), 143.

[10] Sanford Sternlicht, "Introduction." Christopher Fitz-Simon and Sanford Sternlicht (eds.), *New Plays from the Abbey Theatre 1993-1995* (Syracuse: Syracuse Univ. Press, 1996), XVIII.

Ireland, thus representing the larger community: Leo is an immigration officer, Mary has just obtained a law degree, and their father, Bill, a widowed sacristan, has just retired from the service of the Church. The mini-community of the three betrays signs of severe disintegration: suspicion of the other's behaviour, the lack of shared moral convictions, and estrangement from each other, symptomatic of how individualistic ambitions tend to undermine traditional bonds in contemporary Irish society. As widely precedented in dramatic literature, the outsider figure, in this case Joseph, catalyzes the existing tensions and embodies a mirror that reflects and highlights the personal dislocations and needs of the Gaughrans themselves.

Fintan O'Toole contends that the self-perception of the Irish "as a morally pure part of the Third World, as belonging to the oppressed rather than the oppressors" is ruthlessly shattered in the conflicts of *Asylum! Asylum!*[11] The gap between father and son, so often foregrounded in twentieth century Irish dramas as a sign of discontinuity and a site of (post)colonial fragmentation, reaches a critical point in O'Kelly's work over the treatment of Joseph. Bill, on the verge of losing control of his life, is profoundly moved by the refugee's guilt-laden story about how he was forced to contribute to the torture and violent death of his own father, and offers shelter to the young man in his house. The understanding of the two men grows and strengthens as they discover the connections between their worlds, especially as "both their cultures attach a similar importance to the inventing and telling of stories."[12] Joseph's perfect command of Bill's language "contradicts his difference constructed by racism,"[13] and further emphasizes the cultural links because their societies both adopted English from the former colonist as an essential part of hybridization. Like Uganda, Ireland had been a colony of Britain, and the African and the Irishman engage in a kind of "the empire laughs back" game when reciting the rhythmic exclamations of the native servants who were carrying Winston Churchill around in Uganda in a rickshaw during his one-time visit of the country: "Burrulum! Huma! Burrulum! Huma!"[14] Meaning "iron" and "wood," the tandem of the two words suggests creative co-operation between the colonizers building the rails and the colonized providing pieces of wood, yet, ironically, in a language incomprehensible for the colonizer.

The correspondence between the actual experiences of Bill and Joseph is underscored in the text by deploying the same images to describe the sufferings they were exposed to by the respective historical and political events that

---

[11] Fintan O'Toole, "Nationalism hampers real intensity." *The Irish Times,* Aug. 9. 1994, 8.
[12] Heiner Zimmermann, op. cit. 70.
[13] Ibid. 71.
[14] Donal O'Kelly, *Asylum! Asylum!* Christopher Fitz-Simon and Sanford Sternlicht (eds.), op. cit. 158. All further references are to this edition.

affected their lives. Joseph's detailed story of what happened to him and his father back in Uganda depicts the brutality of maiming and destroying humans, both physically and psychologically, by fire and smoke:

> The soldier lit the straw himself. He lit it at four different points. The straw blazed. The logs began to smoke.... Lumps of burning soil fell through the logs onto the men in the pit. They screamed and coughed. Except the older man. He just moved his lips and looked at me. The prodigal son. Returning, laden with gifts. The soldier who took my passport led me to the part of the school where the roof still was. Smoke followed us. (143)

In turn, Bill recollects the North Strand bombing in his country by the Nazis during the war: "May 1941. Mammy gave me a terrible clatter for standing up at the window. The sky was lit by the flames. 'Get back in under the stairs,' she said. Next morning the smell of the black smoke was everywhere" (156). In two different lands, the two men became helpless victims and shocked eyewitnesses of the horrors of imperialist and post-imperialist violence targeting on ordinary civilians.

Paradoxically, it is the very fact of having a lot in common with the asylum-seeker that makes Leo antagonistic to Joseph's plea and makes him use his job of immigration officer to deny the latter sanctuary. Both embody the role of the prodigal son, and together recollect a song, heard from their own fathers in childhood, through which, temporarily, they recuperate the lost harmony of the parent-child relationship. While Leo keeps his reserve, Joseph enthuses over the coincidence: "You see!? People are the same everywhere! Always trying to get the kids to go asleep! The red choo-choo and the blue choo-choo!" (121). "Ireland is a first-world country, but with a third-world memory" in Luke Gibbons' formulation,[15] involving a historically shaped contradiction between two poles, which may trigger schizophrenic behaviour in certain situations. Leo's hostile treatment of Joseph is fuelled by the suppression of his own share of the third-world memory as a corollary to his determination to emigrate and rise in the first world of the continent, working for Europol. He condemns postcolonial Ireland in terms resembling the Yeatsian link assumed between lack of room and hatred:

> ...back biting and back stabbing, I can't stick it anymore. Thank God Nobody gives you credit here. It's small, it's parochial, nothing is decided on merit, everybody knows everybody's past, everybody's out to rattle the skeleton in the other fella's cupboard, it's all nod and wink and who does High-and-Mighty think he is considering where he came from he's only a glorified bouncer ... I'm getting out. I hate it here. (134)

---

[15] Luke Gibbons, "Ireland and the Colonization of Theory." *Interventions* 1. 1 (1998), 27.

The general moral stagnation of the country, Leo adds, deprives the individual from taking a second chance, which seems to explain the fatal collapse of his marriage. Emotionally scarred, he is also a failed father, whose psychic homelessness runs parallel with Joseph's physical one. His ambition to start a new life on the continent reverses the refugee's strife to relocate himself in Ireland, far away from Uganda, where, amidst the postcolonial conflicts, he would surely become the object of revenge taken either by his own community for his inadvertent facilitation of his father's murder, or by the militia's side, who need no witness to the gross atrocities they committed.

Leo, however, makes use of the other's excruciating third-world experience when he successfully acts "the part of an African trying to bust his way into Europe" (135) by repeating what he heard from Joseph for the European authorities. Thus he proves his competence in "understanding the twists and turns of the immigrant's mind when he is trying to squeeze in uninvited" (135), and also his capability of spotting such frauds. Extremely cynical on the surface, the performance discloses a double nature, in that it is a combination of the subaltern's clowning to gain advantage and betrayal of himself by misusing the other, who is, in fact, his double. Before O'Kelly, Thomas Kilroy's Field Day play *Double Cross* (1986) dramatized a similar kind of self-divided Irish performance in the protean behaviour of Bracken, who agitates against foreigners in his speech as conservative candidate to a crowd in England, while keeping his own origin in secret. Resembling Bracken's and Joyce's contempt for their Irish mirror images in each other, Leo's wish is to get rid of the African Joseph, who reminds him of his own homelessness and insecurity. Before actual deportation can be effected, he, frustrated as he is, goes as far as torturing Joseph, at least verbally. In Act II, set in the backyard of Bill's house where Joseph can, at last, enjoy the air of freedom having been released from jail, Leo, while barbecuing meat, stirs up his painful memories by referring to heat and smoke in Africa.

Mary, who undertakes the legal defense of Joseph's case at her brother's not at all unselfish request, seems to be ready to serve an abstract humanitarian cause, although she resents the idea of moving back to her father to look after him. This contradiction in attitude, however, begins to be replaced by warm humanism and the realization of others' needs, once she feels real concern, even love, for her client. The new relationship helps her to understand her father's former coldness toward her, but open conflict with her brother is unavoidable, feeding on their old sibling jealousies and other deeply nursed wounds that surround their opposite views about Joseph's future. Mary's psychologically mediated third world memories are also evoked when Joseph refuses to entertain her with his childhood stories, suspecting that her interest is that of the white woman in the Noble Savage and not in his real person. She proves to be able to identify with him by confessing her feeling of uncertainty and fear, which have accompanied her since her loveless childhood under the care of a grief-stricken, incommunicative father: "... most of the time I'm a messy kind of Mary who's actually weak sometimes in private, and who trembles inside with panic when she looks like she's at her coolest ..." (152). She needs Joseph's stories to heal the painful absence of her own life's little intimacies, indicating her sense of real mutuality in their relationship, devoid of any trace of the potential self/other binarism underlying the (neo)colonial discourse.

Joseph's appeal for asylum is denied after a few months, due to the interference of immigration officer Pillar, Mary's former friend and Leo's colleague, whose officiously taking up action is obviously influenced by jealousy and hatred of "that jungle juice" (150). Yet he tries to arrange the case quietly, asking Mary to persuade Joseph to leave the country in peace, thus to demonstrate humanitarian treatment. In a remarkable verbal battle in the final act Leo, returning from the continent, plays the boss and orders Pillar to implement the most extreme methods of deportation in Joseph's case. When Pillar refrains from such "cruelty," Leo exposes his hypocrisy as being a version of neo-imperialism with a mask, which uses "the carrot instead of the stick" (165) approach of sophisticated colonialist manipulation, but to the same dehumanizing end. During his service in Europe, Leo had the opportunity to see Joseph's story of his father's victimization come to life in Rostock, Germany, where a hostel full of Vietnamese refugees was attacked by an indigenous mob. Based on a real incident which occurred in August 1992, Leo's report teems with the same horrifying tropes that characterized Joseph's story of the violence in Uganda and Bill's memories of Nazi bombing: "The flames reached the top of the stairwell.... I panned across to the last flat. A man stood there, looking out. I felt he was looking at me. The flames burst through the door of his flat. He still didn't move. Smoke filled his room. His lips formed words" (166). His discovery in the statue-like man of both the image of Joseph's father and that of all other victims, as if a monument to inhumanity, is reminiscent of the experience described by Eugene O'Neill's character Orin, home from war: "I had a queer feeling that war meant murdering the same man over and over, and that in the end I would discover the man was myself!"[16] The three violent stories in *Asylum! Asylum!* are connected by manifestations of the racial hatred and intolerance haunting mankind down to our time in various places and in different guises, yet with equal destructiveness. For Leo the experience in Germany serves an eye-opener, its importance enhanced by the particularity of its location, Rostock, the home of citizens who only recently became free from totalitarian rule. In their new situation, postcolonial in a sense, feeling the su-

---

[16] Eugene O'Neill, *Mourning Becomes Electra. Three Plays of Eugene O'Neill* (New York: Vintage, 1959), 305.

periority of West Germans "greatly hinders a development towards more self-confidence in mastering problems without tending to shift blame onto others,"[17] and becomes the hotbed of xenophobia.

Leo's Damascus conversion completes the basis of reuniting the Gaughran family in love, understanding and genuine care for each other. Joseph, who brought them together, is transported back to Uganda, tied up in a bundle called *Kandooya,* meaning "briefcase" in his native language. The Irish authorities, who disbelieve his story about political violence in his country and label him an economic migrant to be expelled, disempower and humiliate him by enacting the same thing that happened in the Bucoro schoolyard. *Kandooya,* the image of the objectified, immobilized, gagged body, both in the Ugandan story and in the Irish deportation event, corroborates the universal threat of what man is capable of doing to man to perpetuate fear from self-protecting power. Like a parable, the play's conclusion offers an antidote to this with the reunion of the Gaughrans through solidarity with Joseph, the foreign other, who functions as a mirror revealing their own crisis and thereby facilitating its resolution. As Julia Kristeva argues, today "we confront an economic and political integration on the scale of the planet" and should discover our own "incoherences and abysses," our own "strangenesses" to become capable of "promoting the togetherness of those foreigners that we all recognize ourselves to be."[18] For the time being, however, like the game of chess between Bill and Joseph in O'Kelly's play, the reconciliation of the "two worlds" of native and alien remains an unfinished business.

The Priest Preaching Racism

In choosing to place the marginalized Leopold Bloom, the son of an immigrant Hungarian Jew in the centre of his monumental epic, *Ulysses,* Joyce was allegedly influenced by the treatment of the Jews in early twentieth century Ireland. He knew about the Limerick pogrom of 1904, the year in which the book is set, and also about the restrictive Aliens Act introduced in 1906; he would also have read the notoriously prejudiced articles published in the wake of the events, among them the ones penned by his adversary, Oliver St. John Gogarty. The upsurge of racism produced "a strong reaction" in Joyce, leading to the creation of Bloom, "one of the strongest and most enduring refutations of anti-Semitism in western culture."[19] In the pub-scene of the "Cyclops"

---

[17] Wilhelm Heitmeyer, "Hostility and Violence towards Foreigners in Germany." Tore Björgo and Rob Witte (eds.), *Racist Violence in Europe* (London: Macmillan, 1993), 26.

[18] Julia Kristeva, "Strangers to Ourselves." Kelly Oliver (ed.), *The Portable Kristeva* (New York: Columbia Univ. Press, 1997), 264-65.

[19] Dermot Keogh, *Jews in Twentieth-Century Ireland: Refugees, Anti-Semitism and the Holocaust* (Cork: Cork Univ. Press, 1998), 56-57.

chapter of the book, Bloom gives an inclusive definition of Irishness and dares to confront the racism of the Citizen, who resorts even to violence in combating an opinion different from his, while he perceives himself as builder of a new Ireland. The persistent mode of Joyce's work being "subversive parody in which he has seized the rules of dominant decolonizing discourse and disrupted what he sees as its flawed identitarian message,"[20] it exposes aggressive xenophobia as compensation for the insecurity felt by the colonial subject. For the Citizen and his drinking pals in *Ulysses*, the foreign element Bloom not only embodies but also defends for its intercultural values, cannot be accepted as part of Irishness, because it does not fit the homogenizing narratives within which they construct their version of national identity.

First performed in 1998, John Barrett's *Borrowed Robes* is a play that, in a way, takes up the thread where Joyce left it. Set in an unnamed Irish city in 1904, its action embraces the persecution of a small Jewish community of East European origin, relying on the documentary material which inquires into the responsibility of Fr John Creagh, director of the Arch-confraternity of the Holy Family, a Catholic order based in Limerick, for the precipitation of incitement against the local Jews. "It would appear," as contended in research findings related to the Jews in Ireland, "that the priest had been approached by shopkeepers in the city who were hostile to the Jewish pedlars because they provided unwelcome competition."[21] Creagh, in his irresistible style of inflammatory preaching, warned people to have no dealings with the immigrants, the campaign he launched resulted in boycott and violence.[22] Barrett creates a priest figure, the similarly named James Keane to be the central character of *Borrowed Robes*, whose attacks on the local Jews are recognizably modelled on the historical Fr Creagh's. Nevertheless, the play is created as fiction, introducing a complexity of socially and culturally entrenched personal motifs to account for the sudden upsurge of racism and its wider implications. While his work undertakes to stir up dormant memories of "a deeply disturbing incident" in Irish history, "John Barrett thinks that the play's appearance now is timely, as hostile attitudes towards immigrants are surfacing again."[23] On the other hand, the clerical figures it stages invite being measured against the implications of the recent scandals bringing into the open "the hypocrisies and failings which have always been present within the Church."[24]

---

[20] Gerry Smyth, *Decolonisation and Criticism: The Construction of Irish Literature* (London: Pluto Press, 1998), 83.
[21] Dermot Keogh, op. cit. 26-27.
[22] Ibid., 30.
[23] Helen Meany, "Skeletons in the Cupboard." *The Irish Times*, 23 July, 1998. 12.
[24] Fintan O'Toole, *The Lie of the Land: Irish Identities* (London: Verso, 1997), 111.

Father Keane's figure and attitudes are abundantly contextualized and motivated in the first part of the drama. Originally from the country, he has retained a keen interest in nature, and several instances demonstrate his uncorrupted, innate goodness: helpfulness and sympathy toward others, concern with children's and young people's welfare, involvement in projects of charity. Sarah Levin, the Jewish protagonist runs a boarding house to which Keane himself is said to have sent lodgers to boost her business. From Scene Two, in which Keane talks to his Superior, Father MacNamara, it turns out that his career has followed a typical pattern in early twentieth century Ireland, where many lower and middle class parents sent a son to the seminary to study for priesthood and in this way raise the socio-economic position and prestige of the family. At the age of twelve, the young man did not have much choice but go along with what was decided for him. In case he abandoned the vocation later, he would be stigmatized a "spoiled priest"[25] by the community, and more often than not became a homeless outcast who had to ponder emigration as a viable solution.

MacNamara denigrates Keane by referring to him as "The single talent well employed" (15), quoting Samuel Johnson,[26] and Keane, indeed, feels he has failed to fulfil what was expected of him, regarding himself a disappointment to his mother despite having risen to the positions of Parish Priest and Master of Novices by his thirties. Once "an average student, perhaps a bit below average" (15) in the wording of MacNamara, who clearly looks down on him, he suffers from an inferiority complex in the clerical job. Urged to make up for this, he takes every rule of the religious order far too rigorously, including extra fasting periods and offering additional sermons. It is his strong sense of duty that engages him in the unrelenting pursuit of Michael Burke, a runaway novice, who left the order for having fallen in love with a girl and found shelter in the young but already widowed Sarah Levin's house. Sarah and Keane have been old acquaintances, and their mutual interest in each other dating back to six years before is tellingly suggested by subtle gestures and nuances in the play. The attractiveness of the woman combined with her kind, genuine concern for Keane's person when he first visits the place in search of Michael, revives his buried feelings. It is the torment of forbidden love that will transform him into a schizophrenic monster who preaches against the object of his passion, the Jewish woman, and her race.

Composed of short, intense scenes, interlocking through juxtaposition and contrast, the play is best described as post-Brechtian, "appropriating the body

---

[25] John Barrett, *Borrowed Robes* (unpublished typescript, Dublin, 1998), 6. All further references are to this copy.
[26] I owe thanks to the author, Dr. John Barrett, for his generous assistance in clarifying the intertextual references in the play.

as the site of sensory interchange with its natural and social environments" and thus phenomenalize the political "to pursue its roots in the personal realities of embodiment and world-constitution."[27] Deploying this perspective, we find that touching, as a sign of bridging the gap between self and other, has a persistent recurrence in the text. The description of Keane in corporeal terms as "virile and energetic" (13), even handsome, foregrounds the problem of the extraordinary effort he has to make to resist the natural needs of the body. Subject to the rules which prohibit a religious to touch and to be touched, the occasions when he checks an impulse to lay his hand on another human being out of sheer sympathy and goodwill reify his profound ambivalence. "A very physical woman" (5), the Jewish Sarah would be a real match for him but, as a sigh she heaves after first calling his handsome figure to mind indicates, she is well aware of the manifold walls separating them, reinforced by Keane's downright rejection when she offers to help him take off his coat. Therefore, the propensity with which she "tends to touch people, quite naturally" (5) can be viewed as a compensation for having also to repress her feelings. Claiming about marriage that "That part of my life is over" (23) signals her sexual frustration, yet her culture and relative social freedom allow her to cope with it in a way directly opposite to the priest's bodily recoil who, in accordance with the internalized principles, represses his love by mortifying the body.

During his visits to the house, the sight of Sarah touching the ex-novice, a bodily intimacy barred to him, is fatally misread by Keane, infuriating him and also raising his jealousy. His deepening personal crisis culminates in the paradox that the woman who embodies the object of his ego's desire becomes the abject of his superego.[28] He dreams of her in private, reciting from the *Song of Songs* in praise of the beautiful feet and captivating tresses of the beloved. In public, however, he chooses Sarah's people as the target of his increasingly ferocious sermons, which vilify the Jews enlarging upon the economic, spiritual, and especially moral threats they mean for the Christians. His being torn apart between duty and desire is physicalized by keeping the purple stole in one pocket of his cassock and Sarah's reddish scarf, which he has snatched from her and worships instead of her body, in the other. Avowing the war of the flesh "against the Spirit" as its contrary following St. Paul (50), he seeks new ways of advancing the victory of the Spirit over the flesh when he employs the spiritual force of the narratives available to his profession, selecting quotes from the Bible as well as from the most biased Church literature and from the anti-Semitic rhetoric of Easter Week. His preaching is eloquent with all his repressed passion trying to express itself through vehement refer-

---

[27] Stanton B. Garner, Jr. *Bodied Spaces: Phenomenology and Performance in Contemporary Drama* (Ithaca: Cornell Univ. Press, 1994), 162.
[28] Cf. Julia Kristeva, "Powers of Horror." Kelly Oliver (ed.), op. cit. 230.

ences to the body as the source of sinfulness, ordering the congregation to terminate all kinds of contact with the Jews.

Sarah enjoys the life of a self-employed, independent woman who dares to disobey male authority and refuses to be married to a widower at the advice of the rabbi because he is personally unattractive, thereby subverting the accepted gender norms of both her own community and the surrounding Irish society. As Keane's awareness of the consuming power of his passionate love poisoned with jealousy heightens, so does he proceed to use the intersecting discourses of race and gender to disparage otherness through its materialization, and, as its contrast, to refigure himself as a spiritualized being.[29] Slandering the carnal charms of Jewish women, now he unmistakably alludes to Sarah:

> Has not our Holy Mother Church given us constant warnings? Have not the Popes and the Saints time and again? ... In London, in Paris, in Berlin the Jewess flaunts herself in the salons of the rich—her long dark hair, her silken dress, her painted lips inviting sin. And at whom does she cast her sidelong glances? It is the Christian youth she seeks. She plies him with drink. She seeks him out to claim his manhood! (*Murmurs*) Why do I talk of Paris, of Berlin? They are here within our own city. There is a young man, not half a mile from here, a seminarian dedicated to God, a novice of our holy Order, ensnared in the clutches of the Jewess. (58-59)

Meeting the woman for the last time, Keane explains his dread of going to work on the Foreign Mission where his Superior has sent him. It is given in a way that masks an abortive love confession: "I cannot say ... To you ... of all people. You don't know? It is not possible. How can you not know? If I live, if I *survive*, through the dark hours of every day and night, it is because ... it is because..." (77). The confused message of the words derives from the oxymoron of the priest's bodily existence threatened by the life-giving force of bodily desire, dislocating his whole subjectivity and making him look like a madman in the eyes of the other characters. Yet Sarah is able to unravel all the mystery and touches him lovingly which he returns, resting his head on her shoulder, though only for seconds. Rushing away, the transgression of the always so conscientiously observed rule of not touching anyone, let alone the loved one out of sexual desire, incites him to deliver the last, most fiercely hostile, because also self-abjecting sermon, a more than ever vituperative declaration of war on the Jews.

In the drama Sarah Levin is the only Jewish character appearing on stage. Open to all parts of the larger community, she has non-Jewish lodgers and claims to have got on well "with Catholics, with Protestants—with everyone" (43) until the time of the pogrom. Her style of life defies stereotyping: her

---

[29] Cf. Stanton B. Garner, Jr. op. cit. 196.

children go to a Catholic school, and her late husband, a sculptor, used to work also for the Catholics, like the Quaker chandlers in Sebastian Barry's *Prayers of Sherkin* (1990). However, whereas Barry's lyrical play transcends all the potential conflicts of the different communities, Barrett's work exposes latent xenophobia, a long-lasting corollary of colonially determined internal divisions and related sensitivities. Racist demagogy, especially because delivered by a representative of the traditionally "rabble-rouser" priests,[30] is capable of reviving suspicions and susceptibility to sensing the enemy even where there is none. Because of the rigidity of the system, the authority figures do not hasten to prevent the unfolding of the pogrom. *Borrowed Robes* uses the superior priest's figure to reveal a leading Irishman's view of the Jews, in an argument purporting to terminate the anti-Semitic campaign of Keane and calm him down by the same stroke:

> Oh, the Jews, the Jews, the Jews. Irritating? God help us. So good at making money, you see—unforgivable. You respect them, but you don't have to ask them to dinner. Very like us, though, in many ways—apart from the drink. Family centred, a strong religious sense, persecuted, forced to emigrate. I mean, basically, what is a Jew? A sober and energetic Irishman. (38)

In spite of its undoubtedly witty turns of formulation, Keane is not altogether wrong to dismiss this mixture of contemptuous prejudice and misplaced eulogy as "offensive" (38). Replete with clichés and stereotypes regarding both the Irish and the Jews, it is obliquely racist, by suggesting that the desirable thing is to see the native identity as the norm, and the immigrant can be accepted and well thought of if s/he conforms to it. Emphasizing the value of uniformity rather than acknowledging the value of pluralism in culture, it implies that foreigners cause the least trouble if they behave like the Irish themselves. Such artificially levelling views concerning multicultural relations as MacNamara's are apt to make ordinary Catholics vulnerable to shifts from one extreme to another, and even turn against their neighbours. However, the drama does not fail to inscribe the problem in the larger context of the colonial society where the natives had been made strangers in their own land by a powerful minority. There is ample manifestation of tensions related to the Catholic-Protestant divide as well as to the authority of Britain over Irish social and cultural politics. The bishop, whose accent betrays Northern origin, concludes his answer to Sarah's appeals for help with the claim that "I know very well what it's like to be ambushed on your way to school" (62). Although he is naturally prompted to sympathize with her plight, he decides not to take immediate action against the both physical and existential humiliation of a minority group

---

[30] Kevin O'Connor, "Audience put on the rack." *Sunday Times,* 9 Aug. 1998, 22.

by controlling his own people. As a result, the racial aggression leads to tragedy, its devastating self-destructiveness well demonstrated by the violent death of Joseph, Michael's brother, an Irishman killed for his respect for truth and outspoken willingness to defend the other community.

The split-minded Keane's tragedy, avalanching more violent tragedies in his surroundings, is intimately linked to the manifold problems within the Catholic Church itself. Having preceded the building of the state historically, it became "a kind of surrogate state"[31] that assumed too much power, creating and maintaining a centralized bureaucratic system. Apart from its original usefulness in colonial Ireland, the latter has facilitated the covering up of several psychologically and morally damaging occurrences, not discussed openly before our time, when the society started to shed the clerical control. The enforced doctrine of priestly celibacy and the Church's rigid puritanism concerning matters of sexuality have contributed to the emergence of several forms of perversion—suffice it to think of the child abuse cases involving priests and Church-run institutions. Sarah's discussion of the Jewish rabbis' obligation to take a wife while they continue to serve God is an example in the play not only of religious differences, but also of the ways in which one culture could reconsider its habits and regulations in view of another. Highlighting another aspect of Jewishness, her story of the Cossacks' murderous attacks on her family back in Lithuania cannot but deeply move an Irishman, as it definitely does move Keane, yet his own trauma proves to be overwhelming and renders him totally myopic.

The "impeccably groomed" (15), smooth-tongued, shrewd and thoroughly secularized MacNamara, and through him the Church itself, bear a great amount of responsibility for the deplorable excesses of Keane's racist propaganda. When the young priest struggles with what he names, as taught, "bad thoughts" (49) and confesses, the Superior absolves him according to Church doctrines but makes no real effort to understand his tormenting despair. As earlier, MacNamara's intention to persuade Keane to take things easy backfires: his story of once having a memorable affair with a Belgian girl shocks Keane as betrayal, adding to his disturbance instead of relieving it. A world in which he believed collapses, burying him even deeper in his unsolvable crisis. The seemingly benevolent, shoulder-patting attitude of the superior priest conceals hypocritical self-centeredness. When Keane's first racist sermon appears in print, his primary concern is how it affects his own reputation: "This is my life's work, Father—trying to show them, trying to show our Protestant brethren that we can be trusted.... I am Chairman of the Cultural Committee of this city!" (35). Living under the conditions of a divided society, however, complicates the picture by implying the difficulties ambitious Catholics met

---

[31] Fintan O'Toole, *The Lie of the Land: Irish Identities*. 65.

with if they wished to achieve wider recognition. Hypocrisy in a priest, exemplified by MacNamara's behaviour, was the complex product of trying to override both the unendurable rigour of religion and the obstacles of self-definition in the colonial world that encouraged mimicry and conformity.

The final scene displays a remorseful Keane in the empty church, reciting the story of Cain and Abel which ends with the question "What hast thou done?" (84). Himself victimized by his own actions, he "takes off his cassock, then his stock and collar" (84) and stands there in his white shirt and black trousers like his runaway novice at the beginning of the play. He discards the "borrowed robes" representing clerical authority that he, undermined by his crisis as a priest, denied the natural, grossly misused. The time being just before Easter, the play does not conclude on total hopelessness: the sacrifice of Jesus carries the possibility of redemption for Keane as well as the community to revise their ways and prevent the horrors of racism and violence from happening again. Several recent Irish plays, as Jochen Achilles writes, probe into the social function of religion undertaking the subversion of dogma, yet ultimately display "a tendency to search for redemptive factors in a world threatened by a total loss of meaning."[32] With its story of suffering and loss underscoring the need for a new approach both to elements of the native culture and to respecting that of others, *Borrowed Robes* well deserves a place in this group.

Conclusion

In the last part of his book on Irish drama Christopher Murray claims that the present generation of young Irish people finds "its preferred liberty in secularism, tolerance, and a new, very appealing humanism," forming part of a "new ethos" which is reflected in the theatre as well.[33] O'Kelly's and Barrett's respective plays are not innovative with regard to form or style, yet they are impressive achievements of the contemporary Irish political theatre because of the novelty of their subject matter and their contribution to the artistic "examination of buried wounds" that goes on in the country.[34] In both, the narratives of the Irish are set against, and fruitfully viewed together with those of other peoples, continuing what Friel started by creating a complex intercultural milieu in his *Dancing at Lughnasa* (1990). Whereas the postcolonial paradigm marks a still relevant approach to *Asylum! Asylum!* and *Borrowed Robes*, these works can also be recognized as belonging to a

---

[32] Jochen Achilles, "Religious Risks in Contemporary Irish Drama." *Eire-Ireland* 23. 3 (1993), 17-18.
[33] Christopher Murray, op. cit. 246.
[34] Helen Meany, op. cit. 12.

"different debate about race, ethnicity, nationality and history," which currently develops in Europe and produces literature that addresses issues of "cultural contact."[35] In Ireland, the ramification of the debate is probably just a natural extension of the postcolonial, modifying its historical entrapment by investing it with comparative strategies that reconfigure the discourses of self and other, native and stranger.

---

[35] Gabriele Schwab, "Literary Transference and the Vicissitudes of Culture." Jürgen Schlaeger (ed.), *REAL: Yearbook of Research in English and American Literature. 12: The Anthropological Turn in Literary Studies* (Tübingen: Gunter Narr Verlag, 1996), 117.

Romanticism, Identity and Intertextuality: Edmund Burke in Late Twentieth Century Irish Criticism and Drama

Introduction

An allegedly catalytic figure in the evolution of British political thinking, the eloquent parliamentarian and philosopher Edmund Burke (1729-1797) is viewed by modern literary histories as a significant precursor of Romanticism. His powerful distinction between the beautiful and the sublime in *A Philosophical Enquiry into the Origin of Our Ideas of the Sublime and Beautiful* (1757), inspired by De Boileau's translation of Longinus on sublimity[1] and pointing forward to Kant's *Analytic of the Sublime* (1790), provided ample stimuli for several English writers of the subsequent decades. Any substantial study of the Gothic attributes a formative role to *A Philosophical Enquiry* in the emergence of that mode of writing, mainly because of its consideration of terror as an aesthetic quality. Burke's later major work, *Reflections on the Revolution in France* (1790) influenced English Romantic writers by its reverance for the imagination and hatred of confining arguments, as well as by its insistence on traditions rooted in spiritual nobility and the nourishing values of the past. Critical research has found Wordsworth's growing admiration for Burke demonstrated most tellingly by direct references to it in the poet's own monumental work, *The Prelude*.[2] Concerning another aspect of Romanticism, parallels between the transformed meaning of the aristocratic for Burke and Byron have been pointed out. Burke invested it with a transcendental quality, whereas Byron re-occupied the term "reinfusing it with its disturbing peculiarity."[3]

Compared to the fame that Burke had earned in England and other European countries by the twentieth century, his reception as an Irish writer in his country of birth, Ireland, has a much shorter, though recently remarkably intensifying history. The causes and processes involved in discovering the Irish Burke are exciting to examine, since his re-appraisal and re-canonisation are heavily underpinned by the implications of Ireland's cultural decolonisation. During the Literary Revival it was W. B. Yeats who expressed profound respect for Burke, describing him as one of the great Protestant intellectuals of

---

[1] Fred Botting, *Gothic* (London and New York: Routledge, 1996), 39.
[2] Tom Furniss, "Burke, Edmund." Jean Raimond and J. R. Watson (eds.), *A Handbook to English Romanticism* (London: Macmillan, 1992), 42.
[3] Jerome Christensen, *Lord Byron's Strength: Romantic Writing and Commercial Society* (Baltimore: The John Hopkins Univ. Press, 1993), 307.

eighteenth-century Ireland. His opinion was shaped, at least to a considerable extent, by Matthew Arnold's attempts to assess Burke as a writer for his nation. The concept of Irish literature, however, became more exclusive for those of their contemporaries who promoted the revival of the Gaelic language and the de-Anglicisation of Irish culture. Douglas Hyde's *A Literary History of Ireland* (1899) declared its intention to draw the literary map of Irish-Ireland, neglecting the works of the Anglicised Irishmen of the past, including Burke, who, for him, belonged to the English tradition.[4] This logic was taken to the extreme later when Daniel Corkery, a highly influential critic of the Irish Free State lumped Burke together with Sheridan, Goldsmith, Wilde, Shaw, Moore and even with Joyce, and described all as expatriate writers "who did not labour for their own people" and the moulds they fashioned could not "express the genius of Ireland in the English language."[5] Corkery certainly sounds narrow by today's postnationalist standards, but after so many centuries of colonialism that suppressed the native culture it was understandable, although not wholly laudable, to emphasise the demand for the purely national.

The limitations manifest in the cultural life of postcolonial Ireland started to disappear only gradually, along with the steps taken toward modernisation and rebuilding links both with Europe and Britain in the 1960s and 70s. Irish literary discourses have been undergoing changes since, in the direction of a greater refinement of aesthetic appreciation, complexity and plurality of views, along with redefining the approach to sectarian and other divides. A new generation of critics entered the scene, who engage in reinterpreting the work of several formerly marginalised or even excluded Irish writers and thinkers of the past centuries. Outstanding among the tangible results of this enterprise we find the three volumes of *The Field Day Anthology of Irish Writing* (1991), which offers the so far broadest selection of historical Ireland's literary output from the early middle ages to the present. "An act of repossession," general editor Seamus Deane says, which is

> ... not merely an exercise in regaining Swift, Berkeley, Goldsmith, Burke, Shaw, Yeats, Joyce, Beckett, and so forth from the neighboring fiction of English or British literature or literary tradition. It is a recuperation of these writers into the so-called other context, the inside reading of them in relation to other Irish writing, in order to modify and perhaps even distress other "outside" readings that have been unaware of that context and its force.[6]

---

[4] See Gerry Smyth, *Decolonization and Criticism: The Construction of Irish Literature* (London: Pluto Press, 1998), 77.
[5] Daniel Corkery, *Synge and Anglo-Irish Literature* (Cork: The Mercier Press, 1931), 7.
[6] Seamus Deane, "Introduction." Terry Eagleton, Frederic Jameson and Edward W. Said, *Nationalism, Colonialism and Literature* (Minneapolis: Univ. of Minnesota Press, 1990), 15.

With regard to Burke himself, the recent studies of Seamus Deane, Conor Cruise O'Brien, Declan Kiberd, W. J. McCormack and others have made efforts to fathom his enigmatic Irishness and redeem his importance for the national heritage. In the following, this paper surveys their contribution to achieving a more varied picture of Burke as an early Irish Romantic, as well as looks at the subtle ways some passages of Burke's work become intertextualised in recent Irish drama.

Burke's Early Work in Contemporary Irish Criticism

Conor Cruise O'Brien's voluminous, highly acclaimed biography *The Great Melody* (1992) is an uncontestable mine of material concerning Burke's ties with Ireland and the sources as well as consequences of his characteristically cleft-minded identity. The book's title derives from a poem by Yeats, some crucial lines of which the author quotes in the "Introduction": "American colonies, Ireland, France and India / Harried, and Burke's great melody against it." The "it" here, as O'Brien explains, means the abuse of power, different though in each cited case, that Burke critiqued in his own writing.[7] "Melody," Yeats's metaphor borrowed, evokes the persistence, poetic strength and Romantic colouring of Burke's writing. Son of an Irish Catholic mother and a father who converted to Protestantism in adulthood pressed by the demands of his career in law, Burke received education first in an Irish hedge-school, then in a Quaker school, and finally graduated from Trinity College Dublin, the highest-degree establishment institution. Thus he became an Irish Protestant, but his family-based connections with the Catholic part of the population were never severed, also because his wife was of that persuasion.[8]

Summarising Burke's career, a critic claims that "Not a very typical Irishman, one would say, and yet Burke was intensely Irish."[9] Paradoxically, entering British service constituted the only opportunity for him to influence colonial policy and improve the conditions of the Catholic majority who suffered under the discriminating Penal Laws imposed after their defeat in the Williamite wars.[10] But this undertaking was bound to result in feeling "threatened by the internal schisms of divided loyalties, or a division between inner loyalty and outward conformity."[11] Not surprisingly, his attempts at maintaining a delicate balance invited malicious attacks from blinkered politi-

---

[7] Conor Cruise O'Brien, *The Great Melody* (London: Minerva, 1992), XXIII.
[8] Ibid., 3-23.
[9] Lorna Reynolds, "Edmund Burke: A Voice Crying in the Wilderness." Okifumi Komesu, Masaru Sekine (eds.), *Irish Writers and Politics* (Gerards Cross: Colin Smythe, 1989), 49.
[10] Conor Cruise O'Brien, op. cit. 39.
[11] Ibid., 30.

cal adversaries time and again. Once the angered William Hamilton, Chief Secretary for Ireland mentioned Burke in his notes as "Jew-Jesuit," doubly alien from Englishness.[12] In order to help the Irish Catholics, as well as in the interest of advancing his own personal career largely to the same end despite inherent difficulties, "detachment and even dissimulation were desirable" for him, besides consciously chiselling the modes of making indirect utterances concerning Ireland in his writing.[13] In short, the unheard part of Burke's melody about his native land tended to sound sweeter than the heard one.

Placing *A Philosophical Enquiry* in the context of eighteenth-century Irish philosophical and aesthetic literature requires critics to measure it against the diversity represented by contemporary writers. Under the title "The Irish Counter-Englightenment" David Berman meditates on the "unique flowering of Irish philosophy between 1696-1757, and for explanation turns to the political background.[14] In eighteenth-century Ireland the colonial situation spawned a double-edged social configuration, which did not fail to impinge on the main currents unfolding in philosophical thinking. The Catholics formed a dispossessed majority facing whom Irish Anglican philosophers like George Berkeley found themselves in an "insecure and precarious position,"[15] and their anxieties poured into works that favoured irrationalism and paradoxes. Catholic-born, Dissenter-turned Irishman, John Toland was prominent among those who formed another tradition, close to Enlightenment ideas. As for Burke, he shared with Berkeley a deep hostility for the deism expounded in Toland's *Christianity Not Mysterious* (1696). However, the subversiveness, duplicity and "esoteric/exoteric strategy" of Toland's later writing, necessarily emerging as it did "to challenge the official discourses of power," recurred in his own works as well.[16] With regard to the past, in accord with Berkeley's refutation of Locke's empiricism, "Burke believed that Locke and his theory of sense-perception ignored the historical dimension, the way in which communities were held together by tradition."[17] Originating from a painfully divided country, Burke developed a keen desire for unity, which led him on to forge the concept of the nation, a key-element of Romantic ideology.

Discussed by Seamus Deane's *A Short History of Irish Literature* (1986), "the powerful role given to emotion, mystery and religion" in Burke's *A*

---

[12] Ibid., 48.

[13] Ibid., 68, 97.

[14] David Berman, "The Irish Counter-Enlightenment." Richard Kearney (ed.), *The Irish Mind: Exploring Intellectual Taditions* (Dublin: Wolfhound Press, 1985), 136.

[15] Ibid., 137.

[16] Richard Kearney, *Postnationalist Ireland: Politics, Culture, Philosophy* (London: Routledge, 1997), 164-66.

[17] Declan Kiberd, *Inventing Ireland: The Literature of the Modern Nation* (Cambridge, Mass.: Harvard Univ. Press, 1996), 322.

Philosophical Enquiry contrasts sharply with the other important treatise born in eighteenth-century Ireland, Francis Hutcheson's *Inquiry into Beauty and Virtue* (1725), which offered a "smug, benevolist" interpretation of the aesthetic and ethical as joint issues.[18] On the other hand, the "sensationalist aesthetics" expressed in *A Philosophical Enquiry* betrays commitment to the eighteenth-century Irish school of theological representationalists. Burke's sympathy for their position was already present in his *Reformer* (1747-48), a miscellany published with the purpose of shaping and reforming public taste. Under the theological representationalists' influence Burke argued that humans understood God's attributes and the mystery of their operation as they came on the mind in the form of sensible images, capable of affecting the imagination.[19]

Burke anticipates a great deal in Romanticism by the thoroughly framed description of "emotions attendant upon the Sublime," while his work is also an extension of Berkeley's "attack upon the limitations of the Lockean theory of meaning."[20] At the same time it is true that, although the Irish philosophers rejected Locke he, nevertheless, managed to turn their thoughts on epistemological questions, and within that "on the nature of perception and on language."[21] Burke's *A Philosophical Enquiry* enriches this line with gripping observations about poetry informed by sympathy and not by imitation, concluding that language not only communicates but raises passions.[22] Burke, in fact, praises poetry for its obscurity,[23] and in Section VII of Part V, titled "How WORDS influence the passions," he elaborates on the immense potential in language to create, stating that "by words we have it in our power to make such *combinations* as we cannot possibly do otherwise" and thereby "give a new life and force to the simple object."[24] Decades later, in a letter to his son Burke discusses the underside of the same question, highlighting the possible manipulation of words:

---

[18] Seamus Deane, *A Short History of Irish Literature* (London: Hutchinson, 1986), 52.
[19] David Berman, op. cit. 135.
[20] Seamus Deane, *A Short History of Irish Literature*, 52.
[21] David Berman, op. cit. 119.
[22] Declan Kiberd, op. cit. 322.
[23] Edmund Burke, *A Philosophical Enquiry into the Origin of Our Ideas of the Sublime and Beautiful* (Oxford: Oxford Univ. Press, 1998), 57.
[24] Ibid., 158.

> A very great part of the mischiefs that vex the world arises from the words. People soon forget the meaning, but the impression and the passion remain. The word Protestant is the charm that locks up in the dungeon of servitude three millions of your people. It is not amiss to consider this spell of potency, this abracadabra, that is hung about the necks of the unhappy, not to heal, but to communicate disease.[25]

Investing language with such world-(re/de)constructing power that anticipates certain tenets of modern European language philosophy has remained central to Irish culture down to our time, as an intellectual-spiritual corollary of the physically imposed colonial situation and its aftermath.

Burke's Later Work in Contemporary Irish Criticism

Burke was working as a Whig party politician during several decades of his life and became famous, for some infamous, by his enormous oratorical talent. His speeches, letters and tracts written in favour of the American revolution, against the abusive colonialist treatment of India and, most importantly, to remove the Catholic disabilities, infuse the language of reasoning with the ambiguities of poetry. The invaluable collection of Burke's nationally relevant shorter writings in *The Field Day Anthology* contains parts of his 1782 "Letter to a Peer of Ireland," in which he dissects the seemingly benevolent proposal of offering education for some Roman Catholic Clergymen in Trinity College. To convey an ultimately negative opinion with compelling density, his method operates by juxtaposing as well as contrasting multiple contexts that surround the same question:

> The act, as far as it goes, is good undoubtedly. It amounts I think very nearly to a toleration with respect to religious Ceremonies. But it puts a new bolt on Civil Rights; and rivetts it I am afraid to the Old one in such a manner, that neither, I fear, will be easily loosend.... I have known men to whom, I am not uncharitable in saying, (though they are dead), that they would become papists, in order to oppress protestants; if by being protestants, it was not in their power (to oppress) papists.[26]

Neither was couching his thoughts in allegorical discourse an unknown path for Burke. In parliamentary speeches concerning oppressive colonial politics in India Burke's empathy with that country under occupation "was also ex-

---

[25] Edmund Burke, from "Letter to Richard Burke, Esq." (1793). Seamus Deane (gen. ed.), *The Field Day Anthology of Irish Writing Vol. I.* (Derry: Field Day Publications, 1991), 848.
[26] Edmund Burke, from "Letter to a Peer of Ireland" (1782). Seamus Deane (gen. ed.), op. cit. 821-22.

pressed in terms which vividly recalled the extirpation of Gaelic traditions by adventurers and planters."[27]

O'Brien comments on Burke's frequent deploying an English persona to represent the author's views on certain political implications or an Aesopian language to clothe his real meaning.[28] Also, his "mastery of cumulative argument" manifests itself in speeches that recommend a kind of policy not by overt references but through the "general tenor" of the text.[29] The passage the biography quotes from at this point is widely recognised for its exceptionally forceful rhetorical embellishments:

> Leave the Americans as they antiently stood, and these distinctions, born of our unhappy contest, will die along with it.... But if, intemperately, unwisely, fatally, you sophisticate and poison the very source of government, by urging subtle deductions, and consequences odious to those you govern, from the unlimited and illimitable nature of supreme sovereignty, you will teach them by these means to call that sovereignty itself in question.[30]

Burke's freedom-supporting attitude to the affairs of America, India and Ireland may make it seem surprising that his *Reflections* condemns those who overthrew the monarchy and introduced a new order in France. The contradictory position of the work is highlighted by Novalis, the German Romantic poet in the most positive terms: "Burke has written a revolutionary book against the Revolution."[31] Digging deeper in its ambiguities, Seamus Deane discusses the debt of *Reflections* to Montesqieau, whose political text both Burke and the revolutionaries reinvented according to their respective desires.[32] The importance of Montesqieau for Burke lay in the latter's describing "the old feudal laws of the Franks in such a way as to make it plain that he favoured the recovery by the contemporary aristocracy of the privileges which had been lost under the despotic rule of Louis XIV."[33] On the other hand, *Reflections* is a work where Burke, an Irishman, by the comparisons he makes between the revolutionary French and the conservative English systems,

---

[27] Declan Kiberd, op. cit. 17.
[28] Conor Cruise O'Brien, op. cit. 196.
[29] Ibid., 143.
[30] Qtd. Ibid., 143-44.
[31] Qtd. in W. J. McCormack, *From Burke to Beckett: Ascendancy, Tradition, and Betrayal in Literary History* (Cork: Univ. Press Cork, 1994), 28.
[32] Seamus Deane, "Montesquieu and Burke." Barbara Hayley and Christopher Murray (eds.), *Ireland and France: A Bountiful Friendship* (Gerards Cross: Colin Smythe, 1992), 29.
[33] Ibid. 21.

defines the nature of English freedom to the English, emphasising the role of continuity without which "things lose their substance."[34]

Though it does not include any mention of Ireland, *Reflections* tends to be seen in recent Irish criticism as a text which, under the mask of political literature, unmistakably joins itself to the national heritage. Declan Kiberd claims that "the threat to traditional sanctity and loveliness was evoked by Burke in the image of ravaged womanhood."[35] This effect is achieved by the richly imaginative, nostalgic recollection of Maria Antoinette and her disastrous fall:

> It is now sixteen or seventeen years since I saw the Queen of France, then the Dauphiness, at Versailles; and surely never lighted on this orb, which she hardly seemed to touch, a more delightful vision. I saw her just above the horizon, decorating and cheering the elevated sphere she just began to move in, — glittering like the morning star, full of life, and splendor, and joy. Oh! What a revolution! and what an heart must I have, to contemplate without emotion that elevation and that fall! ... I thought ten thousand swords must have leaped from their scabbards to avenge even a look that threatened her with insult. — But the age of chivalry is gone.[36]

Employing this strategy Burke, Kiberd continues, cast himself in the role made familiar by the visionary *aisling* poems evolving in eighteenth-century Ireland, which allegorised the country in the figure of a defenceless woman yearning for liberation.[37] Elsewhere, in his miscellaneous writing Burke "contended that what happened to the native aristocracy in Ireland under Cromwell and the Penal Laws befell the nobility of France in the revolution of 1789: an overturning of a decent moral order."[38]

Upon more reflection about the fineries of *Reflections*, McCormack asserts that bringing together politics and aesthetics "in a conjunction of the most profound significance" the work, from the outset, "attracted attention to its language."[39] The great house, edifice and building recur as dominant metaphors in the Burkean text. This imagery, however, often assumes a tone of irony, underscoring the contrast between the ruination caused by revolutionary experimentation and "a wholeness which historical community may afford."[40]

---

[34] Robert Welch, *Changing States: Transformations in Modern Irish Writing* (London: Routledge, 1993), 17.
[35] Declan Kiberd, op. cit. 17.
[36] Edmund Burke, *Reflections on the Revolution in France*. L. G. Mitchell (ed.), *The Writings and Speeches. Volume VIII: The French Revolution 1790-94* (Oxford: Clarendon Press, 1989), 126-27. All further references are to this edition.
[37] Declan Kiberd, op. cit. 18.
[38] Ibid., 17.
[39] W. J. McCormack, op. cit. 29.
[40] Ibid., 39.

For example, The Constitutional Committee of the National Assembly is referred to by Burke as "the French builders, clearing away as mere rubbish whatever they found, like their ornamental gardeners, forming everything into an exact level," but whose work of measurement soon needed "another basis (or rather buttress) to support the building which tottered on that false foundation" (220-22). Deane's latest book locates the unique strength of *Reflections* in uniting diverse literary modes and styles. Visibly constructing itself on eighteenth-century epistolary and travel literature, Burke's masterpiece contains, Deane argues, "chivalric passages" about the queen and the royal court absorbing the traditionalist specular mode of looking which focuses on the emblem, opposed to the revolutionary way of applying the speculative lens.[41]

Recuperating *Reflections* for the Irish literary heritage, Seamus Deane justifiably calls it "the first of Ireland's national narratives," a text "in which the notion of a national, anti-modern narrative becomes a governing principle."[42] And this anti-modernism of Burke, while undeniably preparing the ground for the Romantic in general, had an impact on the traditionalist approach of many later Irish writers. The Celtic Revival of nineteenth-century Ireland, to overcome historical wounds, recovered the distant past for the idea of a once strong, heroic and noble kingdom on the land.[43] In the process of this dreaming back the Burkean images of the ruined building, contrasted qualities, theatricality and mystery "were incorporated into the literature of Thomas Moore, Sir Samuel Ferguson and, in an etherealised version, of James Clarence Mangan, thereby leading to the promotion of a sense of Irish cultural identity."[44]

Contemporary critical inquiry answers further questions concerning Burke's legacy as a shaping force in the cultural nationalism of the last decades of the century. The Irish founder of British nationalism, Burke had an English advocate in Matthew Arnold, who edited an anthology titled *Edmund Burke on Irish Affairs* (1881) to clarify Burke's role in highlighting the problems of Ireland. This compilation embodied an influential contribution to the unfolding second wave of the Revival.[45] Updating Burke's thoughts, Arnold, Deane adds, "gave fresh emphasis to the sectarian features which were part of the Irish political situation by providing them with a cultural myth."[46] To deepen the ironies of Irish cultural developments, this romanticising of the Celt be-

41 Seamus Deane, *Strange Country: Modernity and Nationhood in Irish Writing since 1790* (Oxford: Clarendon Press, 1997) 11.
42 Ibid., 25.
43 Seamus Deane, *A Short History of Irish Literature*, 56.
44 Seamus Deane, "Edmund Burke and the Ideology of Irish Liberalism." Richard Kearney (ed.), *The Irish Mind*, 151.
45 Seamus Deane, *Celtic Revivals* (London: Faber and Faber, 1985), 24.
46 Ibid., 27.

came appropriated by revolutionary nationalism to idealise the Irish Catholic, in a way that neither Burke nor Arnold had envisaged. But nationalism, as pointed out by postcolonial criticism, is but an offspring of colonialism, involving the mimicry of the master. Absurd as it may sound,

> The construction of a continuous, unaltered tradition, stretching back to remote antiquity can be seen, in fact, as precisely a colonial imposition, an attempt to emulate in an Irish context the Burkean model of the English constitution based on an organic theory of community and the inherited wisdom of the ages.[47]

To complete the picture let us remember that the last Romantic, first modernist Irish poet, Yeats, venerated Burke for the wrong reasons when placing him in the pantheon of the Protestant Ascendancy. It was a class that Burke detested, and may have been much astonished to see his own name beside that of Grattan in the gallery of pride Yeats allocated for them in his monumental poem *The Tower*.

Burkean Texts in Contemporary Irish Drama

Some of Burke's ideas, especially through their relevance to the problem of postcolonial Irish identity occur in late twentieth-century Irish drama that often uses intertexts, literary as well as theoretical, to widen the intellectual scope and reach beyond its characters' immediate mental grasp. Burke himself might have welcomed this warmly, as he had immense admiration for the theatre as a social form of art, capable of revealing important truths. In a letter he wrote: "A History of the Stage is no trivial thing to those who wish to study Human nature in all its shapes and position ... The Stage indeed may be considered as the Republick of active Literature."[48] Crediting these assumptions with literary practice, images of the theatre abound in his own later work. *Reflections* refers to "such a profane burlesque" (119) when characterising the national assembly set up by the revolution and to "the Supreme Director of this great drama" (131) when discussing the debasement of royalty. Even the "theatric audience in Athens" would hardly be able to endure the sight of what the actors on the French stage are performing (132). "In the theatre," Burke expounds, "the first intuitive glance, without any elaborate process of reasoning, would shew, that this method of political computation would justify every extent of crime" (132).

---

[47] Luke Gibbons, *Transformations in Irish Culture* (Notre Dame, Indiana: Univ. of Notre Dame Press in association with Field Day, 1996), 157.

[48] Qtd. in Michel Fucks, *Edmund Burke, Ireland, and the Fashioning of Self. Studies on Voltaire and the Eighteenth Century, 353* (Oxford: The Alden Press, 1996), 199.

Not accidentally, Burkean lines appear as intertexts in two such plays, Brian Friel's *Philadelphia, Here I Come!* (1964) and Thomas Kilroy's *Double Cross* (1986), where the characters' split-mindedness is foregrounded along with their attempts to combat feelings of insecurity and search for ways to renew their identity. *Philadelphia* is set in a small Donegal county town in the early 1960s, on the eve of the young protaginist's planned emigration to the USA. Throughout the play Gar O'Donnell continues to appear in two forms, as Public and Private, representing the interplay of the objective and the subjective sides in his character. Public "behaves" and talks to others in the clichéd language of the puritan environment, while Private acts, gesticulates and monologises, conveying the dreams and fantasies fermenting inside the boy but remaining unexpressed openly. Several times, Gar quotes the first few words or lines of Burke's nostalgic description of Maria Antoinette from *Reflections*. Without any logical link to the surrounding text, the refrain-like outbursts seem to externalise unconscious desires, especially as it is Private, the subjective part who echoes the borrowed words. Considering the points of its occurrence in the drama, Anthony Roche rightly suggests that the quotation is intimately associated with Gar's dead mother and the loss of his girlfriend, and thus with his craving for love and nostalgia for the feminine.[49]

Friel's play, however, highlights the split between two sides also on the national level. Gar confronts the choice between traditional Ireland and the call of the modern world, America with its promise of bright lights and unbridled opportunity. And the former means a good deal more than the experience of real communication drowned in clichés, painfully evident in Gar's talks with his father, and the impossibility of rising socially. It means home, and the rhythmic intrusion of the Burkean text about the beauty of the past poeticises Private Gar's memories and reconfirms his rootedness in old Ireland. Contrasted with it is Public's frequent singing of a version of the title-giving song, which merrily embraces the idea of emigration: "Philadelphia, here I come, right back where I started from."[50] The words of the song, however, run a circle: arriving in a place not different from the point of departure suggests that life under his aunt's stifling hospitality in the City of Brotherly Love will hardly redeem Gar from his present problems. Wedged between the seductive haunting of the nostalgic narrative of the past and the fragile, deceptive promises of the future, both Gars, Public and Private, appear hesitant about how to go on at the conclusion of the play. As if performing the situa-

---

[49] Anthony Roche, *Contemporary Irish Drama from Beckett to McGuinness* (Dublin: Gill and Macmillan, 1994), 93.
[50] Brian Friel, *Philadelphia, Here I Come! Selected Plays of Brian Friel* (Washington, D. C.: The Catholic Univ. of America Press, 1986), 44. All further references are to this edition.

tion of Ireland itself in the early 1960s, at the threshold of a new era of its development.

Thomas Kilroy's *Double Cross* was written for the Field Day Theatre
Company, based in the double-named border-town of Derry to be a forum for
the presentation of dramatic works exploring questions of Irishness. Following
the company's main goals, Kilroy's play uses two, subtly complementary historical figures: Brendan Bracken from a nationalist and William Joyce from a
loyalist background, who both left their country for England in the 1920s. The
former began to work for Churchill's information service, while the latter
became known as Lord Haw Haw, broadcasting fascist ideology for the British
from Nazi Germany. In the play the two, though they never actually met,
"become mirror images of each other, each self-made man craving the
integrated community each idealises in the English imperium."[51] Played by the
same actor on stage, their difference of sectarian background represents the
nation divided. Psychically affected by the inculcated doctrine about the inferiority of the colonial other, they reject their Irishness. However, condemning
their country of origin and insisting on an artificially fabricated national identity entangle both Bracken and Joyce in multiple self-divisions and betrayals.

In Burke's phrase, Catholics under the penal code found themselves as
good as "foreigners in their native land."[52] Elaborating on his childhood spent
in still colonial Ireland even if over a century later, Bracken complains about
feeling the same: "… I used to imagine, as a little boy, that people didn't
recognise me, that I appeared to everyone as a stranger."[53] Trying to mas-
querade as British, he seems to consider Burke as a model to follow, having
the Romney portrait of the politician-writer dominate his living room (17). To
justify his choice of a new identity he resorts to the Irishman Burke's praise of
the British inheritance: "To be bred in a place of estimation, to see nothing
low or sordid from one's infancy — to be habituated in the pursuit of honour
and duty—" (37). The following excerpt from the play, however, testifies to
Bracken's gross misreading of Burke to endorse his own exclusivism deriving
from the contempt for Ireland:

> BEAVERBROOK Ah. You know Gandhi once quoted Edmund Burke at
> me. You know—the Indian. The one who wants to
> dismantle the Empire. Do you know Gandhi, Brendan?

---

[51] Christopher Murray, "Worlds Elsewhere: The Plays of Thomas Kilroy." *Éire-Ireland* 29.2
(1994), 134.
[52] Luke Gibbons, op. cit. 176.
[53] Thomas Kilroy, *Double Cross* (London: Faber and Faber, 1986), 36. All further references
are to this edition.

BRACKEN   … I don't need to know him. I know his type….
             Determined to prove the superiority of the primitive. I
             would happily trample him into the ground. What do
             these people know of law? Of grace? Cultivated living?
             They would overrun us, mark you. With their foul
             smells. Their obscene rituals. Animalism. (37)

And yet another Burkean resonance surfaces in a distorted fashion here. Burke
himself saw parallels between India and Ireland, and when criticising British
colonial policy he even forecast the possible end of the empire through corruption and imagined the return of the repressed in the form of an animal.[54]
However, he never felt or expressed hostility toward the colonised inhabitants.
In fact, as Kiberd goes on, "Burke contested English stereotypes of the Irish
… but he believed that, taken together, the English and the Irish had the mak-
ings of a whole person."[55] Bracken's quoted remarks cast an ironic light on
his predilection for Burke as he, largely out of key with the master, does everything to deny his belonging to Ireland and its traditions.

By mimicking the imperial oppressor both Bracken and Joyce just exacer-
bate their being burdened by the damaged colonial psyche which they so ve-
hemently wish to abandon. The personal trauma of Bracken is reinforced by
the feeling that a brother figure, in fact his double haunts him. Desperately
fearing this other in himself, he condemns the brother as a criminal who has
stolen the portrait of Burke from over the mantelpiece in his living room. In
this context, Bracken's misinterpretation of the Burkean legacy and its self-
destructive consequences warn against acts that privatise meanings and turn
identity into a hollow fiction, disregarding its complexity. By way of contrast,
Kilroy included in his drama lines from W. B. Yeats's *Innisfree,* a poem articulating its writer's dream to leave England for Ireland and live near its waters and birds, reminding the audience of Yeats's cultivation of an Irish identity.

Coda

The vividness discerned in the critical and intertextual journey of Burke on the
map of late twentieth-century Irish culture indicates a continuing presence and
impact. His work conceived under the various pressures of Ireland's colonial
peculiarities, the real Burke, of course, remains elusive like all truly great
writers. His both enigmatic and paradoxical Irish/Britishness and classicist-
tinged Romanticism are, however, just the very qualities that make his work
today so attractive in his native country that can, at long last, afford to realise

---

[54] Declan Kiberd, op. cit. 18.
[55] Ibid. 19-20.

the need to reconcile itself to and also benefit from its historically shaped ambiguities. As an article published in *The Irish Times* on 31 December 1998 claims:

> ... the year which expires today is the greatest in Irish history, for it has seen the triumph of ideas over tribalism, and the final victory of freedom over the tyranny of violence. The ideas are those of Burke ... who spoke endlessly of the need for political arrangements to reflect the reality of the flawed nature of the people who must operate them. That man is the greatest political philosopher the Irish and the British peoples have produced: Edmund Burke. His hour has come.[56]

---

[56] Kevin Myers, "An Irishman's Diary." *The Irish Times,* 31 December, 1998, 15.

Part Three

The Identity of Plays

"We All Have Our Codes. We All Have Our Masks": Language and Politics in Brian Friel's Stage Version of *Fathers and Sons*

Turgenev's Novel

Though he chose to spend a considerable number of years elsewhere like many an Irish writer after him, Turgenev is said to have maintained a lifelong interest in the socio-political issues of his troubled home country, Russia. His *Fathers and Sons* (1861), as critics have discussed, is justifiably a novel of its times. The conflict between the liberal and radical views, and the problems such a conflict involved, could not but provoke a landowning writer into presenting his own artistic comments. The novelist created a multilevel narrative, with a young Nihilist intellectual, Bazarov, in the centre, in which the social and the political concerns establish a frame within which the intricacies of individual ideas and feelings are richly elaborated.

According to David Lowe's analysis, "Turgenev's judgement on his age is ambivalent, but not ambiguous."[1] The fact, however, that the novel can still be regarded entirely modern, prompts scholars to look for its secret outside the generation conflicts of the last century. A large part of Turgenev's strength appears to lie in his ability to reveal that a human being is always more than the codes s/he uses and the masks s/he wears: Henry James rightly pointed out his ironic but tender treatment of the individual.[2] At first sight, Bazarov's Nihilist convictions appall, but before long his tragic vulnerability is exposed because "the circumstances of social transition and his own ideas isolate him even from himself."[3] Viewing Nihilism as "a pathological transitional stage," Friedrich Nietzsche might have categorised Bazarov with those Nihilists in whom "the productive forces are not yet strong enough, or ... decadence still hesitates and has not yet invented its remedies."[4] The irretrievable loss of his possibilities through dying too early turns him into a tragic figure and the novel transforms itself into a story about the mysterious workings of fate.

---

[1] David Lowe, *Turgenev's Fathers and Sons* (Ann Arbor: Michigan, 1983), 83.

[2] Henry James, "Ivan Turgenieff." Morton Dauwen Zabel (ed.), *The Portable Henry James* (New York: The Viking Press, 1958), 460.

[3] David Lowe, op. cit. 90.

[4] Friedrich Nietzsche, *The Will to Power*, trans. Walter Kaufmann and R. J. Hollingdale (New York: Vintage Books, 1968), 14.

Fathers and Sons in the Friel Canon

Friel's stage version of *Fathers and Sons* (1987) follows his translation of Chekhov's *Three Sisters* (1981) and his original play, *The Communication Cord* (produced 1982, published 1983). The connection between the two Russian works as translations in several different senses is evident enough. But though Friel's *Fathers and Sons* is a translation, both in language and genre, and not an original work, a number of scholars have already demonstrated that its themes fit very well into his artistic vision. Ulf Dantanus, for instance, stresses that the main thematic strand in the play can be identified as "the question of loyalty and love, of blind loyalty to a cause and personal loyalty to family";[5] and its entangled picture of generation problems is analysed by Marilyn Throne.[6] According to Richard Pine, *Fathers and Sons* is "about homecomings, like the ones made by Frank Hardy and Owen O'Donnell."[7] "With Bazarov, Friel presents his definitive outsider figure," George O'Brien contends, and it is he who includes the play in the group under the heading "Friel's Theater of Language," since it gives voice to "the discrepancy between the apparent finality of language and the flux of non-verbal areas of being."[8]

However, these critics do not mention that it is not only themes but also the motifs, scenes and shreds of conversations from earlier plays that echo in a recognisable form on the pages of *Fathers and Sons*. Nikolai Kirsanov's words, "We all have our codes. We all have our masks." (Act I, Scene 1)[9] seem to reflect the remark made in *Living Quarters*, "We all have our regrets."[10] Nikolai's and Anna's discussion over the map of the Kirsanov estate in Act II, Scene 1, where an "old well" is pointed out (49-51), is powerfully reminiscent of Act II, Scene 1 in *Translations*. Vassily Bazarov's account of past actions, including his son's funeral in Act II, Scene 1, recalls the basic story-telling situation in *Faith Healer*. In the final scene of *Fathers and Sons*, Ben Jonson's poem "To Celia" is sung and generates some debate about who actually wrote it, reminding us of a short conversation in *Aristocrats*, where the alcoholic Alice begins to sing the same poem and Eamon tries to have Tom, the chronicler, believe that reciting it was a memorable, repeated event in his childhood. The merry singing of Nikolai and Katya is counterpointed by

---

[5] Ulf Dantanus, *Brian Friel: A Study* (London: Faber and Faber, 1988), 212.

[6] Marilyn Throne, "The Disintegration of Authority: A Study of the Fathers in Five Plays of Brian Friel." *Colby Library Quarterly*, 24.3 (1988), 171.

[7] Richard Pine, *Brian Friel and Ireland's Drama* (London and New York: Routledge, 1990), 201.

[8] George O'Brien, *Brian Friel* (Boston: Twayne, 1990), 115.

[9] Brian Friel, *Fathers and Sons* (London: Faber and Faber, 1987), 16. All further references are to this edition.

[10] Brian Friel, *Living Quarters. Selected Plays* (London: Faber and Faber, 1984), 214.

the silence of Fenichka and Arkady at the very end of *Fathers and Sons*, while in *The Communication Cord* the curtain falls on a silent pair and the loud cries of the others. Such echoes not only place *Fathers and Sons* in Friel's canon, but also suggest that adaptation is a kind of interpretation, as, according to George Steiner, are all reading, acting, reviewing and editing.[11] The interpreter makes the text his own by filtering it through his established vocabulary and culturally informed codes.

It is probable that the unfavourable response of most London reviewers after the première of the play in the British capital was due to the fact that, instead of finding the play anchored in one central theme, they attempted to test Friel's faithfulness to the complexity of the novel.[12] What I am attempting to elucidate in this essay is that *Fathers and Sons*, while remaining a "free adaptation"[13] of the novel, qualifies as another of Friel's plays about language. In doing so, I will elaborate on what was suggested by George O'Brien and draw inspiration also from Richard Kearney, whose analysis of *Faith Healer*, *Translations*, and *The Communication Cord* in "The Language Plays of Brian Friel" is a detailed treatment of how the playwright has managed to produce "not just a theatre of language but a theatre about language."[14] In his exploration of what this particular group of plays conveys about the mystery of language, Kearney, supported by quotes from Friel's prefatory programme note to *Translations*, uses aspects of Martin Heidegger's philosophy.

Language as Theme

In regard to *Fathers and Sons* as a whole, it is striking that some of its characters talk a great deal more than the unfolding of the action requires. There are few pages in the play without references to understanding and misunderstanding, hearing, verbal accuracy, or interpretations of former conversations and allusions to the difficulties of communicating private concerns. In addition, the reader is constantly challenged to compare the way characters speak with what they actually do. Nikolai Kirsanov's words, quoted in the title of the present essay ("We all have our codes. We all have our masks."), call attention to communication and identity as the play's central issues. Although I do not intend to claim that Friel deliberately used any of Heidegger's theories, it seems

---

[11] George Steiner, *After Babel: Aspects of Language and Translation* (Oxford: Oxford Univ. Press, 1975), 26-27.

[12] See the reviews by Robert Hewison ("The Problems of Paternity") in *The Sunday Times,* 12 July 1987; Peter Kemp ("Illegitimate Child") in *The Independent,* 11 July 1987; and Julian Graffy ("Remaking Russia") in *TLS,* 17 July 1987.

[13] See Michael Ratcliffe's review of the play in *The Observer,* 12 July 1987.

[14] Richard Kearney, "The Language Plays of Brian Friel." *Transitions: Narratives in Modern Irish Culture* (Manchester: Manchester Univ. Press, 1988), 123.

to be helpful for the purpose of this paper to refer to certain aspects of them. Heidegger's seminal work, *On the Way to Language*, maintains that:

> Speaking is at the same time also listening. It is the custom to put speaking and listening in opposition: one man speaks, the other listens. But listening accompanies and surrounds not only speaking such as takes place in conversation. The simultaneousness of speaking and listening has a larger meaning. Speaking is of itself a listening. Speaking is listening to the language which we speak.... If speaking, as the listening to language, lets Saying be said to it, this letting can obtain only in so far—and so near—as our own nature has been admitted and entered into Saying. We hear Saying only because we belong within it.[15]

Later in the same chapter ("The Way to Language") we can read Heidegger's famous pronouncement that "Language is the house of Being, because language, as Saying, is the mode of Appropriation."[16] Our inference must be that speaking without at the same time properly listening will result in isolated talk, and the lack of real, meaningful self-expression.

In *Fathers and Sons*, the possible entrapment by using a certain kind of language can best be seen in the main character, Yevgeniy Bazarov. On his very first appearance, in the house of his friend's father, Nikolai Kirsanov, "he senses that he is an outsider politically and socially" (8). From this position he speaks with seemingly firm conviction, condemning all that is part of the still existing order in Russia. He is curt and defiant, for instance, when he gives the following retort to Pavel Kirsanov, his conservative opposite:

> Words that come so easily to lips like yours—liberalism, progress, principles, civilisation—they have no meaning in Russia. They are imported words. Russia doesn't need them. But what Russia does need—and action will provide it, Pavel Petrovich, action, not words—what Russia does need is bread in the mouth. But before you can put bread in the mouth, you have got to plough the land—deep. (12)

In terms of language, Bazarov's greatest problem is his aiming "for verbal consistency," which leads to the fatal outcome that he "is both humanised and victimised by his inability to overcome its inconsistency."[17] His initial statements about the need to remake Russia are gradually contrasted with his mixed feelings about the people who make up the country. In Act I, Scene 2, in an outburst to Arkady on the estate of his father, he sounds extremely harsh and

---

[15] Martin Heidegger, *On the Way to Language*, trans. Peter D. Hertz (San Francisco: Harper and Row, 1982), 123-24.

[16] Ibid., 135.

[17] George O'Brien, op. cit. 97.

contradictory: "He [old Bazarov] thinks he loves those damned peasants. I know I hate them. But I know, too, that when the time comes, I will risk everything, everything for them ..." (44).

A series of personal disappointments (Anna's rejection, fighting a duel with Pavel in spite of his beliefs, concentrated in Act II, Scene 1) later leads Bazarov back to the verbalised conviction that he is a dedicated revolutionary: "I am committed to the last, mean, savage, glorious, shaming extreme" (67). His sights, as he prophetically declares, are "trained on a much, much larger territory" than the field of everyday happiness chosen by Arkady (68). This repeated attempt at consistency, however, is rendered meaningless by his going home and becoming involved in curing the peasants he claims to hate until, ironically, he occupies the small territory of a grave instead of the vast one which he referred to in his politically charged language.

The other area where Bazarov suffers a similar defeat is in that of personal feelings and relationships. At the end of Act I, Scene 1, to the genuine consternation of Arkady, his Nihilist acolyte, Bazarov ridicules romantic love and reduces the relationship of man and woman to "a quick roll in the hay—great fun—goodbye" (20). In the next scene he denies the individual differences which form the basis of our distinctive relationships by saying: "We are like trees in the forest ... know one birch, know them all" (25). He mocks the story of Anna Odintsov, the rich widow who escaped into marriage with a decrepit aristocrat, calling it a "rags to riches novelette" (29). But like his political statements, all this remains mere words, because Bazarov's nascent love for Anna annuls the sincerity of both his contempt and his mockery. Verbal consistency is completely laid aside when he asks for Anna's forgiveness for offending her.

Bazarov's gradual entanglement in a web of verbally induced contradictions is checked only occasionally and momentarily by his desperate efforts to use his Nihilist voice again: "Am I in love with this Anna Odintsov? And the answer is: I don't believe in love, in falling in love, in being in love" (37). Yet only a little while later he confesses his passionate love for her (54). The unbridgeable chasm between his earlier, derogatory statements about love and his self-categorisation as a Nihilist, and his human capacity and need for love becomes wider and wider. It implies double defeat—he does not keep faith with his own words and he is accused of misreading "the whole thing" by Anna (54). His marked inability to convey his feelings, because he is not used to employing this kind of language, and his failure to win Anna have the same roots. As George Steiner argues: "Eros and language mesh at every point. Intercourse and discourse, copula and copulation, are sub-classes of the dominant fact of communication."[18]

---

[18] George Steiner, op. cit. 38.

In his *Observer* review, Michael Ratcliffe correctly observes that "scattering its effects through the play, he [Friel] renders the unresolved relationship between the young Bazarov and the beautiful landowning widow Anna Sergeyevna ... even more puzzling than before."[19] It appears to be less "puzzling," however, if it is considered against the backdrop of language and communication as fundamental issues in the drama. The sustaining resource of friendship is also closed to Bazarov because he rejects Arkady after the latter's failure to remain a consistent Nihilist. But his words "that's not how real change, radical change is brought about, Arkady. The world won't be remade by discussion and mock battles at dawn" (67) equally lay bare his own failure.

Bazarov's views on language itself are also turned inside out during the play. In Act I, Scene 2 his Nihilism has him say that "in our remade society the words stupid and clever, good and bad, will have lost the meaning you invest them with, will probably come to have no meaning at all (26). A further distrust of the vocabulary of the old regime is expressed in Act I, Scene 3: "My mother's nice. My father's nice. The lunch was nice. Your uncle Pavel is nice. I've no idea what the word means" (44). Since language and people are inevitably connected, his flat words also admit his ambivalence towards those they refer to or describe. In the same conversation, however, the gap separating his remarks and his behaviour is discovered by Arkady (45). A different link between Bazarov's creeds about language and his personal relationships manifests itself when, through his search for understanding and love, he discovers the value of some previously detested words. In Act II, Scene 1, after Anna's rejection, Fenichka's presence informs him that if, in a particular context, he lets words come spontaneously, they will again be meaningful:

> That's a strange word for me to use—blessed. Six months ago I would have said the word had no meaning ... I think it's because you generate goodness. That's another strange word for me. And suddenly it has meaning, too. You're equipping me with a new vocabulary, Fenichka! (56-57)

Through his unidentified feelings for this girl, who could make a wonderful partner for him if circumstances allowed it, he realises that permanent values do exist in the world and in the word. Again, his personal experience negates the formulations of his political tenets about the devaluation of the inherited vocabulary.

These three main threads tie the figure of Bazarov in a knot of his alienation and his inability to live according to the constraints of a language imbued with political ideology. His tragedy is that he adopts a restricted language as his own and sticks to it in order to overcome his vulnerability. The employ-

---

[19] Michael Ratcliffe, op. cit.

ment of this false remedy results in his isolation, and the structural device used by Friel to demonstrate this is to stage two long final scenes without him. He last appears in the uncommonly long leave-taking ritual (or mock-ritual) of Act II, Scene 2, where his saying good-bye becomes a minor event because all the others are preoccupied with their own concerns. Bazarov's isolation is completed by his untimely death, his unobtrusive withdrawal from a world where he aimed at the impossible by trying to sustain a style of speech and belief even though it continued to be out of touch with his real feelings and actions.

In Turgenev's novel, Bazarov's basic opponent, which becomes clear in their decisive duel, is Pavel Kirsanov, the idle and foppish aristocrat. In Friel, Pavel's language invites a comparison with that of the young Nihilist. As he is in favour of the existing order and all that entails, it is established right from the start that whatever Pavel says is a challenge to Bazarov. However, there is a striking similarity between the two, since Pavel's words do not seem to be coming from him either, but rather from the anonymous patterns of speech and thought he has picked up and absorbed in his worldly progress. His asides in French and "gold-medal bletherskites"-like phrases (12) are good examples of this. The clichés and impatient provocations of his language show him to be a user of and hardly ever a contributor to the verbal treasury. But it is his good fortune that he has much less in him to conceal than Bazarov. Nevertheless, it is to his credit that at the end of the play he confesses that what he has just said to Anna is "the only threadbare wisdom I have for you. I don't believe a word of it myself" (87). As Robert Tracy writes in his review of *Fathers and Sons*, both Bazarov and Pavel can be regarded as outsiders, although in Friel's version the figure of the latter remains weak.[20] This weakness probably derives from the fact that the Irish version places less emphasis on the Romantic-Nihilist opposition than the original does.

Language as Fate

As Friel's *Fathers and Sons* is chiefly about language, the figure who represents a discourse opposed to Bazarov's gains equal significance, and, without doubt, this is Nikolai Kirsanov, who produces a markedly different kind of speech. Nikolai, belonging to an older generation, is a man moved by the political reforms going on in the country—he has already freed his serfs and now is trying to reorganise life and work on his estate. His progress with this task is slow and confused, since he lacks the necessary amount of expertise and self-confidence. This makes him, on the whole, responsible for most of the

---

[20] Robert Tracy, "Brian Friel: *Fathers and Sons.*" *Irish Literary Supplement*, Autumn 1988, 13.

comic moments in the play. The way he speaks and what he says are of special interest whenever he is present; his slogan could be the frequently heard "Now to organise our lives" (8), stemming from his obvious inner confusion. Shapeless sentences, repetitions, jumping from one topic to another, going back on half of what he said a second before, non-sequiturs, asides, needless excuses, missed cues and tag questions pepper his speech almost all the time. Quite often he misunderstands others in spite of his general kind-heartedness, most notably at the end of Act I, Scene 1, when Fenichka, on hearing his proposal of marriage, starts to cry:

> Fenichka? Fenichka, what's the matter with—? My God, what have I done wrong? Did I do anything?—Did I say anything? Did somebody hurt you? Who hurt you? Please don't cry Fenichka. Please. Tell me what's the matter with you. Fenichka? Fenichka? (33)

Nikolai's absent-mindedness often expresses itself in combination with various features of his speech already mentioned: for example, at the end of the play when he refuses to accept that the author of the song he loves is not Shakespeare but Jonson (91).

Nikolai is filled with uncertainty—he gropes for words and often becomes verbose as if wanting to convince himself first of all of the presence of order and decorum in the world. His speech at Bazarov's departure is highly characteristic of the above. "We'll all miss you—won't we? I'll miss all those early morning walks we had—occasionally. And Pavel will miss those—those —those—stirring political discussions" (17). Uncertainty, on the other hand, makes him seek the approval and advice of those around him, for instance his son's in Act I, Scene 1, in connection with Fenichka, and in Act II, Scene 2 when he is listening to what Anna has to say about managing his farm. His too frequent calls for Piotr, the punk-style young ex-serf of his household, and his irritation at the lad's absence or supposed absence are a standard joke in the play. Obviously, Piotr's services are not really what he requires, but he does need to satisfy, in a greatly altered situation, the desire still to act the part of the master and to call for, to upbraid and to reproach someone who is under his authority. Ambiguous feelings are couched in this kind of verbal behaviour.

With all the conflicting tones in his language, Nikolai is closest to adequate self-expression in Friel's *Fathers and Sons*. As David Halliburton argues, ambiguity in the philosophy of Heidegger is an important quality of poetic thinking and "an essential characteristic of Dasein's basic relation to others as well as to itself."[21] Nikolai's speech, tottering as it is, tells more about him and his relation to the world than Bazarov's and Pavel's better formed sentences can ever do. It is not accidental that Nikolai is fond of the arts, plays the cello and sings Ben Jonson's poem in the final scene. "Poetry, as language in the primordial sense,"[22] becomes for him the ultimate means of conveying what is deep inside, even though he himself has not written it. However, not everyone joins in the chorus at the end of *Fathers and Sons*, and no universal release from tension is achieved. The future seems to remain uncertain.

True to the novel, Bazarov expresses great admiration for Nikolai quite early on in the play (17), so the audience cannot discern any hostile opposition between the two of them. It is Nikolai's language which differs from Bazarov's, since it is not undermined by his feelings and actions. Whereas, most of the time, the young man uses direct political rhetoric or statements related to it, Nikolai's words tend to come from the larger realm of his whole being. Despite this difference, both draw on the political atmosphere of the day, in which slogans are as characteristic as the groping for words and uncertain volubility. In a sense, their characters can be seen as contrasted yet also complementary, inviting comparison with other male pairs in Friel's work who represent the unreconciled sides of national and/or individual identity.

While in Bazarov's fate Friel emphasises the tragic aspects of the pressure of politics on human language, Nikolai represents the comic or even clownish aspect, which becomes particularly prominent when, in addition to what we hear from him, he appears in the closing scene wearing a motley jacket. In harmony with his behaviour, he remains on the stage and although he repeats old blunders, at the same time he tries to transcend them. On the other hand, Bazarov displays the danger imbedded in certain ways of using language, which, finally, makes him a victim of an inability to find the way to healing self-expression. He is painfully aware of this problem as well: "I always found it difficult to express exactly how I felt," he tells Anna (53). As a character, Nikolai is not superior to Bazarov at all; he simply represents another kind of discourse, which, though not bringing about tragedy, has the disadvantage of lacking governing principles.

An extreme version of this kind of verbosity is demonstrated in the compulsive talking of Bazarov's father, who seems to have hardly anything to communicate apart from his unease and lack of understanding. Friel, however, does not simplify. The old man also embodies the complexity of human communication as he, on the one hand, hides his grief in the seeming neutrality of words, best exemplified in the narration of his son's funeral:

---

[21] David Halliburton, *Poetic Thinking: an Approach to Heidegger* (Chicago and London: The Univ. of Chicago Press, 1981), 57.
[22] Ibid., 3.

So we buried him on Monday morning, early. A quiet funeral; his mother, Father Alexei, Timofeich, myself. And Fedka, the worthy Fedka, properly shod. It was nice of him to come. And brave. A few prayers. Flowers. The usual. I'll take you there if you wish. (78)

In a genuinely moving way, the scene concludes with a *Te Deum* sung by old Bazarov and his wife in memory of their son, as an expression of "implicit and unquestioning faith" and "their abiding faith in the comfort of their love for each other." [23]

The language of Arkady, Bazarov's Nihilist fellow-student, takes a middle position between his friend's and his own father's. In Act I, Scene 1, he makes extensive use of the Nihilist vocabulary, which leads him to be as talkative as his father. As the play progresses, he displays uncertainty and hesitation as well, and gradually abandons the language of political creed almost altogether. His occasional and faint attempts at resuming it develop from his remorse at his friend's death. "And in the coming years I'm going to devote my life to his beliefs and his philosophy—to our philosophy—to carrying out his revolution," he says, but the declaration remains unconvincing (91-92). By the end of the play, as in the novel, he has proved to remain his father's son. Nevertheless, we can perhaps guess that Arkady's confused transit from the song to the fellow-revolutionary outburst in the closing scene presents a stage just before he develops a style of discourse in which verbalised principles and self-expression both have their place without limiting each other's scope.

Friel's focus on language in this play, as in his others, is a proof of "absorbing contemporary European thought." [24] The dichotomy of verbal ideologising and unbridled, sometimes even empty talkativeness, is displayed in *Fathers and Sons* as a plague of modern life. With this, Friel emphasises an issue which for Turgenev in the nineteenth century had not yet manifested itself so forcefully. In twentieth-century Ireland (and in many other places) there is a danger of the language of politics moving away from the essential needs of ordinary human life. The latter is far more complex than the verbal simplifications which more often than not are political in the broader sense of the word. In Elmer Andrews's opinion the play "dramatises the failure to bring the forces of tradition and modernity into any kind of meaningful dialogical rapport." [25] And this can be identified as a still haunting problem in Ireland.

---

[23] See Richard Allen Cave's review of *Fathers and Sons* in *Theatre Ireland*, 13 (1987), 49.
[24] F. C. McGrath, "Language, Myth, and History in the Later Plays of Brian Friel." *Contemporary Literature* 30.4 (1989), 535.
[25] Elmer Andrews, *The Art of Brian Friel: Neither Reality Nor Dreams* (London: Macmillan; New York: St. Martin's Press, 1995), 199.

A Hungarian Parallel

In 1989 a Hungarian stage adaptation of Turgenev's novel was published by playwright Károly Szakonyi under the title *Nihilisták (Nihilists)*,[26] and given its première in Pécs the same year. In his writing Szakonyi had always been particularly sensitive to the undercurrents in Hungarian social life during the decades of "socialism" before the political changes in 1989, decades dominated by the imposition of an official verbal account of the country. However, the real state of oppression was all too clear to those who cared to think. An indirect or disguised portrayal of lying, apathy and double morality appeared in a wide range of literary works during this period, including Szakonyi's best play, *Adáshiba (Break in Transmission, 1970)*. His *Nihilists* uses the conflict between generations to point to their failure of communication and the resulting loss of values. In the two years before 1990, Hungary had the unique atmosphere of a political transition which left its mark on Szakonyi's play as well. In an unpublished letter he claims to have stressed "nihilism" in order to draw attention to the new Hungarian generation's burnt-out state of mind, due to the lies of their elders. His choice of a Russian work for dramatic reinterpretation is not unprecedented in his career and is comparable to Friel's case, since a few years before completing *Nihilists*, he had already adapted Gogol's *Dead Souls* for the stage.

Szakonyi's *Nihilists* is opened by Bazarov with a Prologue in which the young man fiercely attacks the rule of lies and the devaluation of meaning in language. He says he has become nihilistic along with other young men through witnessing the fathers' corrupt behaviour and becoming tired and depressed with their empty phrases. This critical initial speech has no parallel in Turgenev or Friel and, at least to Hungarian ears, it bears all the hallmarks of an assault on what in early 1989 was still the contemporary one-party political scene. At that time the major debates were taking place between the orthodox politicians who considered the system reformable, and those who were in favour of an entirely new start. The bulk of the play emphasises the clash between slogan-repeating reformers and those who saw the need for total transformation of life and politics.

In addition to the inner conflict that Friel, following Turgenev, allows to emerge in Bazarov, the Hungarian version has him reveal the hypocrisy of the other characters as well. Szakonyi presents the failure of the reformers in the weakness of the older generation and in the comfort-seeking corruption and betrayal of Arkady. Here the fathers are much older than in the original or in Friel, Nikolai being 57 and Pável 60, a change which underlines the timeliness

---

[26] Károly Szakonyi, *Nihilisták. Gondviselés Csevelyszolgálat* (Budapest: Magvető, 1989). All further references are to this edition, translated by the author of the paper into English.

of the Hungarian play: so as to demonstrate their responsibility, Szakonyi may have needed figures who had been born before the communist regime. In this version Nikolai Kirsanov leads the consolidated life of a landowner seeking a friend in his son, with whom to share his problems. Arkady does not offer much help, since he wants to live well and undisturbed. The relationship drawn between these two characters suggests that under the circumstances the younger generation tends to turn out worse than its elders.

Anna's refusal to give herself and her slowness in getting rid of her self-deceptive scruples urge an overall change in personal behaviour as well. Instead of the fragility of the scanty reforms, what is emphasised is the necessity of viewing everything in a new light. Szakonyi's curtain falls on the dying Bazarov, whose loss is felt to have much larger implications than the merely personal, since he could have been a leader of social and political rebirth. According to Anna's closing lines over his deathbed, the unfolding of a better future has been frustrated by human cowardice and conformity: "You did not fit into the world, you had no place in it ... I did not dare to love you. I was wrong.... We could even have had children, brave, strong, and perhaps happy children ..." (191). It was the limits of freedom, in more than one sense, that led to such a far-reaching tragic loss.

Szakonyi's *Nihilists* departs from Turgenev's novel more than Friel's play does, which is indicated by the change of title. It retains and reinterprets more of the political content of the original than Friel's, although it has less to say about language. It was, no doubt, influenced by the transitory nature of the contemporary situation in Hungary and the political debates going on during its inception. The author of its Irish counterpart had not experienced a comparable change in his immediate world, and his adaptation reaches toward more universal implications. The parallel existence of these two different approaches in Ireland and in Hungary seems to indicate that writers all have their own codes and masks, with the help of which they reveal their unique picture of our world, where language, art and politics are crucially involved and connected with each other.

Rewriting the Reread: Brian Friel's Version of Turgenev's *A Month in the Country*

Introduction

Since Julia Kristeva so convincingly persuaded us that "tout texte se construit comme mosaique de citations, tout text et absorption et transformation d'un autre text,"[1] we seem to have had an ever increasing awareness of the relevant significance of adaptations, versions and retranslations of older literary works. By most recent scholarship these have been treated as cases of intertextuality.[2] Due to its complex nature, the genre of drama offers a treasury of examples for adaptation from the ancients to the postmoderns; more than a hundred years ago Dion Boucicault already risked the claim that plays were not written, only rewritten.[3] The playwriting of our times, however, proves especially abundant in diverse forms of this kind of intertextuality. In Ireland the process is particularly intensified as the Hiberno-English transcriptions of mainly classical, French and Russian plays tend to undermine, alter or pluralise established meanings and "by interpreting non-Irish material for Ireland they hope to provoke questions about the condition of Ireland."[4] In his very timely version of Sophocles' *Antigone*, Tom Paulin has the Chorus Leader draw attention to his speech (and the whole play itself) repeating a former one with a renewed emphasis: "Ever since the day I first made this speech—it was in another time and place, and in a different language too—the grief I was speaking of then has grown and multiplied."[5] The catalysing role of the now passive Field Day Theatre Company that first performed *The Riot Act* in 1984 is an undeniable fact of theatre history.

There is, however, another aspect of the issue that should deserve more attention than it has been paid so far. The writer involved in retranslating and adapting assumes the role of a re-reader at the same time, which fact undoubtedly influences his efforts to win other readers and spectators for a particular dramatic work. Nowadays, when reception stands so much in the centre of critical interest, a very characteristic strategy manifests itself as the author not

---

[1] Julia Kristeva, *Sémiotiké: Recherches pour une sémanalyse* (Paris: Editions du Seuil, 1969), 146.

[2] Cf. relevant chapters of Ulrich Broich und Manfred Pfister (hrgs.), *Intertextualität* (Tübingen: Max Niemeyer Verlag, 1985).

[3] Qtd. in Micheál Ó hAodha, *Theatre in Ireland* (Oxford: Basil Blackwell, 1974), 15.

[4] Eamonn Hughes, "'To Define Your Dissent': The Plays and Polemics of the Field Day Theatre Company." *Theatre Research International*, 15. 1. (1990), 72.

[5] Tom Paulin, *The Riot Act* (London: Faber and Faber, 1985), 35.

only aims at renewing a text for its audience but also redirects, rechannels its reception.[6] In his analysis of Friel's *Fathers and Sons*, Richard York points to this effect when claiming that "the motivation of the translator's shaping of the text ... must lie in the world of translator and audience, rather than in that of author and characters; that the translator is saying to us, in essence, 'This is what Turgenev means—*for us, now.*'"[7] In composing his earlier adaptations from Russian literature, *Three Sisters* and *Fathers and Sons*, Friel consulted several existing translations as well as translated between genres, respectively. His *A Month in the Country* (1992) followed a different path, described in the preface as a "very free version" made from a literal translation.[8] The deservedly great audience success of this play may also testify to the possibility of taking a further step in the field of translator/audience co-operation with the rereading rewriter's conscious forming of the text so that it provokingly addresses the contemporary Irish public. Therefore Friel's *A Month in the Country* appears to be the very play that challenges one to look at it in the receptionist context. I proceed on the assumption that in reshaping the material the author was influenced by both his role as a reader and his wish to rechannel others' reading and understanding of the original work. In the following discussion of the play I shall rely mainly on Hans Robert Jauss's principles about reception.[9]

Dialogue Between Work and Audience

The established dialogical nature of the literary work is reinforced in Friel's *A Month in the Country* by consciously facilitating the communication between work and audience. A couple of decades earlier Arthur Miller, who also used a literal translation from another language in his venture of adapting Ibsen, wrote the following: "I have attempted to make *An Enemy of the People* as alive to Americans as it undoubtedly was to Norwegians, while keeping it intact. I had no interest in exhuming anything, in asking people to sit respectfully before the work of a celebrated but neglected writer."[10] Similarly, Friel created a version that speaks to the Irish people of the nineteen nineties in a

---

[6] See Bernd Schulte-Middelich, "Funktionen Intertextueller Textkonstitution." Ulrich Broich und Manfred Pfister (hrgs.), op. cit. 216.

[7] Richard York, "Friel's Russia." Alan Peacock (ed.), *The Achievement of Brian Friel* (Gerrards Cross: Colin Smythe, 1993), 166.

[8] Brian Friel, Preface to *A Month in the Country* (Loughcrew, Oldcastle: The Gallery Press, 1992), 7. All further references are to this edition.

[9] Hans Robert Jauss, *Toward an Aesthetic of Reception*. Translated from German by Timothy Bahti (Brighton: The Harvester Press, 1982).

[10] Henrik Ibsen, *An Enemy of the People,* adapted by Arthur Miller. Ed. Geoff Barton (Singapore: Longman, 1993), VII.

way that involves them and demands a fresh response. Firstly, the sometimes tediously long original had to be shortened to produce a "livelier, nervier, sharper, brisker"[11] work for the sake of the contemporary audience. Changing a series of minor details, the world of the play became more familiar and recognisable as well. Among these the use of the characters' first names or even nicknames (for example Aleksey, the young tutor calls Vera Baby Face) becomes immediately noticeable along with their interaction flowing far more informally than it could have in Turgenev. The scenes between "lovers" are orchestrated with an emphasis on intimacy, the open expression of sexual attraction to show them in an authentic enough light on the present stage. In Friel's Act I, as soon as the players leave the card-table, "MICHEL *takes* NATALYA *in his arms from behind*" (28). With Turgenev, he only presses her hand to accompany his sentence: "At last we're alone."[12] Natalya's confession of love to Aleksey leads to the young man's pressing and kissing the former's hand in the older text, while the infatuation of one and the admiration of the other in Friel is stressed physically: "*He embraces her and swings her round*" (83).

In creating/evoking added as well as new resonances among its audience, Friel's *A Month in the Country* strengthens and often radically modifies the effect of the protagonists' emotional tensions, confusions, jealousies and frustrations in several movements of the play. As usual, the writer's most effective means is his masterful use of language in providing nineteenth-century Russian characters with late twentieth-century nerves and instincts, bridging the gap between them and their audience. In an early talk between Natalya and Rakitin, Turgenev underlines the closed, stale and fragile nature of their relationship by introducing the thought-provoking simile about lace-work:

> NATALYA PETROVNA   ... Do you know something, Rakitin: You're, of course, very clever, but... *(She pauses.)* ... sometimes when we're discussing things it's just as if we were making lace ... Have you seen how they make lace? In stuffy rooms, always sitting still ... Lace is beautiful but a glass of cold water on a hot day is very much better. (6)

---

[11] Robert Tracy, "After Turgenev." *The Irish Literary Supplement* (Spring 1993), 21.

[12] Ivan Turgenev, *A Month in the Country*, translated and edited by Richard Freeborn (Oxford, New York: Oxford Univ. Press, 1992), 18. In want of a literal translation of the original, I have chosen to use the latest, modernised but fairly loyal English translation for comparison. All further references are to this edition.

In the Irish version, the same passage becomes expanded into an embittered comment on human self-centeredness and the accompanying general lack of concern for others. The repetition of "stitches" here as well as at other points in the play connotes an effect that bruises mainly the soul:

> NATALYA I get really angry when you talk like that, Michel. Because you're not talking to me at all: you're playing a private little game of your own. You're like those lace-makers in those gloomy, airless rooms—each one totally isolated, totally concentrated on those minute, complex, subtle little stitches. As if nothing in the world mattered but those ridiculous little stitches. (21)

Only a few pages later, Friel has the ever confused Arkady Islayev's language betray the fact that in spite of his occasional emotional outbursts he has no distinctive interest in his wife: he uses the same adjective ("astonishing") with reference to her and his latest plaything, the new winnowing-machine.

The young tutor's frustration over having lost his Eden and being compelled to choose exile because of unknowingly generating rows and rivalry among those he respected, is well underlined by Turgenev. From describing how the whole situation scares him, here Aleksey Belyaev goes on to speak of escape: "Believe me, Vera Aleksandrovna, I can't wait for the moment when I'll be galloping off in a cart on the main road. It feels stuffy in here, I want to be outside in the fresh air" (126). It is a very appropriately worded refusal of the lace-workers' "stuffy rooms," bound up with Natalya's world of feelings and relationships. (The language of Isaiah Berlin's 1981 translation rendering this as "I'm suffocating here, I want to be out where I can breathe."[13] was not yet so conscious of the parallels.)

Friel's young man expresses his anger as well as disappointment in people: "... I'm so far out of my depth, Vera, I can scarcely breathe.... honest to God I never want to see any of them ever again" (100). In the same farewell scene, Turgenev's tutor convinces Vera that he will never forget her. In contrast, Friel's Aleksey appears both outspoken and unromantic when leaving her with "But it was a good month, too, Vera, thanks to you.... Terrible to think we'll have forgotten it all by Christmas" (101).

The insightful, though embittered, remarks of Michel Rakitin often become charged with new shades of meaning in Friel's version. In the original, his encounter with Natalya immediately following the woman's passionate love-confession to Aleksey, shows him sensitively aware of her change and desire to turn over a new leaf without him. Turgenev's Rakitin comments on

---

[13] Ivan Turgenev, *A Month in the Country,* translated and introduced by Isaiah Berlin (Penguin Books, 1986), 118. All further references are to this edition.

Natalya's behaviour saying "Yes, it's done with. How annoyed you must be now ... for being so frank today, I mean" (108). Friel expands the same interaction of the two by making Natalya rudely negligent of the man's emotional upheaval. He responds using a cynical, Wildean turn:

> MICHEL That's the trouble with baring your soul, isn't it? You regret it
> later. All that inflated language, the emotional palpitations, the
> heaving passions. I've done it so often myself, —in my
> foolishness. It occured to me a while ago that we regret most of
> the things we say and we regret even more all the things we don't
> say; so that our lives just dribble away in remorse. (84)

A few instances of Friel's rearrangement of the original action facilitate the audience's concentration on the actual progress and outcome of the story. Natalya's inner change and confused unhappiness is well demonstrated by a kind of mental jumpiness. Unlike Turgenev, where the topic is more properly introduced and after a pause, in Act One, Scene Two, Friel has her ask Michel about Bolshintsov too abruptly, which at the same time ironically betrays her maturing plans to get rid of Vera. The original's Bolshintsov remains quiet on his appearance later in the same scene, while with Friel his cunning idiocy becomes unmasked in how he, very soon after Natalya's inquiries, resolutely intrudes himself on her: "I'm not a man of much style or grace. So if I can come straight to the point, I'm here because I want—" (48). The presentation of Vera's intended in this aggressive light underscores the reasons for the girl's unfolding disillusionment as well as anticipating the bitterness of her fate—topics as important in Friel's play as Natalya's self-centered greed.[14]

The psychological motives of the tutor's disappointment and final decision are also carefully suggested by Friel's departures from the original's action. In his Act One, Scene Three, Arkady and his mother are accompanied by Aleksey when they find Natalya and Michel in desperate embrace. Subsequently, she remains alone with the young eye-witness and feeds him with an uncalled-for, cynical explanation, presented, according to the writer's instructions, in an "icy, imperious" way: "It's called a domestic scene. You've seen a few in your time, I'm sure, when your father came staggering home from his labouring job" (70). Friel's other novelty is letting her make plans for an intimate rendezvous with Aleksey right after Michel announces his pending departure from the house in Act Two Scene Two. The young man, now even more convincingly, is made to see and become disgusted by how easily she dismisses people in a coldly calculating, peremptory manner:

---

[14] Cf. Robert Tracy, op. cit. 22.

NATALYA   Typical Michel. Totally unpredictable. God alone knows what
           goes on in that strange head of his. Now. Give me your
           hand.... This afternoon I'm going to visit my old nanny at a
           village called Spasskoye. It's about fifteen miles from here.
           And you are going to drive me. And we are going to have a
           picnic together on the bank of the—He suddenly winces and
           withdraws his hand. (96)

In the final scene of Friel's play there is, again, considerable departure from
the original when Anna, Arkady's mother tells her son about a well guarded
secret of her one-time married life which was based on mutual love: "And all
the years we were married, at the beginning of every month ... he went to
Moscow for three nights; to sell timber or grain; or to buy new horses or
equipment. And to visit a lady there that he loved" (89-90). Arkady, listening
to the love-triangle story, is in a seriously disturbed state, having witnessed an
intimate scene between his wife and friend, Rakitin. Although in both
Turgenev and Friel, the husband has been aware of the relationship for a long
time, the fact of its becoming more public carries a shocking effect. With the
help of the above summarised story, and his Arkady's stressed use of the word
"discretion," Friel strengthens what Turgenev merely suggests: in the modern
world keeping up appearances at all cost has become a number one require-
ment in the field of normal social behaviour. This kind of normality, along
with the reestablishment of the usual order of things, however, fails to satisfy
as the Irish Natalya, again in addition to Turgenev's text, expresses it answer-
ing Vera's words of consolation: "For God's sake can't you see it's the normal
that's deranging me, child?" (103).

Conditioning Reception

The literary work, says Jauss, is loaded with "familiar characteristics, or implicit allusions," and "awakens memories of that which was already read,"[15]
thereby conditioning its audience's reception. In the case of the Irish *A Month
in the Country* this process takes place with double force. As its reader, Friel
must have approached the original with other texts in mind which enriched his
subsequent rewriting. A possible example offers itself early in the play, with
the pampered, restless Natalya's outburst of "Oh God, I want—I want—I
want—" (19) concluding in her command that Michel Rakitin resume reading
their book. The same words can be found in Turgenev as well, but for today's
audience the repetition may easily carry an echo of Saul Bellow's Henderson's
modern egocentrism and disquiet expressing itself in an endless *"I want, I
want,"* before he embarks on his quest for the Self. The book the couple reads

---

[15] Hans Robert Jauss, op. cit. 23.

in Turgenev is the romantic *The Count of Monte Cristo*, which Friel replaces with the subtly comic Anglo-Irish novel, *Tristram Shandy*, well known for its challenging of its readers' response throughout. The sentences Michel reads out from its page 115 even testify to a kind of manipulation: "'I have dropped the curtain over this scene for a minute—to remind you of one thing and to inform you of another. What I have to inform you comes, I own, a little out of its due course—for it should have been—'" (19). Friel's use of a number of puns like the one in Natalya's sentence, "My energetic husband—the dam enthusiast" (19) or the Doctor's, "That's the way with those (winnowing) machines: some you winnow, some you lose-ow" (97) adds further Irish tints while underscoring prevailing contradictions in the characters' emotions and the movements of the play at the same time.

In the original, Natalya suggests that she and Rakitin should together finish the shy tutor's education: "It's a splendid opportunity for upright, sensible people like ourselves! We are very sensible people, aren't we?" (9). Friel's Natalya's plan runs like this: "We'll complete his education! That'll be our game for the summer: Polish the Tutor!" (23). "Game," recurring here after Natalya's above quoted poignant comparison of their talk to lace-making in stuffed rooms with Michel employing private games of his own, is an established key-term of social psychology in reference to human behaviour. Edward Albee's *Who Is Afraid of Virginia Woolf?*, a play full of vicious games, naturally comes to mind and our view of Natalya's and Rakitin's relationship tends to be somewhat affected by the memory of the protagonists' tension and cruel treatment of each other in it.

Most penetratingly, however, can the reader feel the haunting of Beckettian texts in Friel's *A Month in the Country*. Echoes of Beckett can be heard in his earlier work as well, suffice it to mention the parallels between *Krapp's Last Tape* and *Philadelphia, Here I Come!*, *Play* and *Faith Healer*. Friel's new Russian play uses the motif of storytelling in a recognisably Beckettian fashion. In Act One, Scene One, the arriving Doctor is expected to give Natalya a good laugh. Turgenev has him recount a long story of emotional entanglements and lack of self-understanding, not at all alien to the woman's state of mind, which starts her thinking. In its place, the two brief stories told by Friel's Doctor die in the awkward silence of failed communication (24-25). Later in the play, recalling *Endgame*, Michel curtly remarks about his jokes: "They're getting worse, Doctor" (85). Arkady appears to suffer from an amnesia to some extent reminiscent of *Waiting for Godot*, as he keeps on misremembering Aleksey's name and obstinately calls him Ivan. However, Friel's context remains concrete: too self-conscious and unbalanced, his ever-busy Arkady proves incapable of having enough respect for others' individuality.

As the reader adds his own experiences and mental contents to the work while processing it, the new version of *A Month in the Country*, born out of Friel's reading and retranslation, naturally bears various signs of similarity to his own artistic world. In turn, his audience is most likely to approach it with several other Friel texts in their memory. In fact, the new play abounds in such details, engaging the readers/spectators in a heightened intellectual activity because their understanding becomes complicated by earlier constructed meanings.[16]

Irish musicality has found its way into most of Friel's works for the stage, and *A Month in the Country* is no exception, much like his other adaptation of Turgenev, *Fathers and Sons*. (True to Turgenev as well in a way, since he was very musical.) In *A Month in the Country*, Friel has Vera play the Irish romantic composer John Field offstage at the beginning of Act One Scenes One and Three and then at the closure of the whole work. On the one hand, music again underlines Vera's significance by making her innocent character's presence felt, often in contrast to the goings-on, even when she remains physically absent. Appearing the way it does, another aspect of the role of music is structural, as in other Frielean and contemporary Irish plays as Henry White discusses them.[17]

Patrick Burke's claim that "The most readily perceivable musical strategy in the plays of Friel is that of commentary, most regularly for purposes of irony or pathos,"[18] finds justification in the case of Friel's *A Month in the Country* as well. At the opening of Act One Scene Three the Doctor's and Michel's discussion of the boorish Bolshintsov's marriage plans concerning Vera, which both of them support, is ironically counterpointed by the fineness of the girl's offstage playing. The same scene ends with Natalya's unbalanced self-questioning about whether to send the beloved tutor away or let him stay and give in to her passion for him. The Field nocturne resounding at this point offers a pathetic accompaniment. Indicating the storm in Vera's soul, Friel's Act Two lacks the girl's music until the very end, when, as a sign of reconciliation to her fate, she plays again with the smiling Bolshintsov, her repulsively unsuiting, fat and middle-aged suitor, listening. The word he repeats, "Nice … Nice …" (109) is the one Bazarov dismisses for its irrelevance so sardonically in Friel's *Fathers and Sons*, in speaking to his friend, Arkady: "My mother's

---

16 Cf. Michael Worton and Judith Still (eds.), *Intertextuality: Theories and Practices* (Manchester and New York: Manchester Univ. Press, 1990), 12.

17 Henry White, "Brian Friel, Thomas Murphy and the Use of Music in Contemporary Irish Drama" *Modern Drama,* 33. 1 (1990), 553-62.

18 Patrick Burke, "'Both Heard and Imagined': Music as Structuring Principle in the Plays of Brian Friel." Donald E. Morse, Csilla Bertha and István Pálffy (eds.), *A Small Nation's Contribution to the World. Essays on Anglo-Irish Literature and Language* (Debrecen: Lajos Kossuth University; Gerrards Cross: Colin Smythe, 1993), 43-44.

nice. My father's nice. The lunch was nice. Your Uncle Pavel is nice. I've no idea what the word means."[19] The emptiness of the word recalled this way, together with the fact that "nice" is such a standardised cliché in contemporary (Americanised) English, lends the play's coda a note of ambiguity.

Occasionally, Natalya or Michel remain alone to struggle with their contending thoughts and feelings. In contrast with the lengthy soliloquies Turgenev involves them in at these points, Friel's version renders their inner debates in brief, staccato-like sentences. They address themselves in the second person far more frequently than in the text of Turgenev, which change calls Gar O'Donnell from *Philadelphia, Here I Come!* to mind,[20] underscoring in turn the split-mindedness of the two characters. In Act One Scene Two the deserted and by now sufficiently suspicious and jealous Michel's self-calming "Steady, man." (46) echoes Private's "Steady, boy, steady."[21]—uttered in warning to the passion-ridden Public of the memory section where he woos Kate who never marries him.

At the beginning of Act Two, Scene Two of Friel's *A Month in the Country*, the agitated and tense Arkady has an argument with his servant, Matvey, from which it turns out that the land-stewart is engaged in "updating survey maps," reminding of the central action in *Translations*. There it serves as a mask for the cultural invasion of Ireland by Britain, during which the old Gaelic names are replaced by English ones. With this in the background of reception, the occasional mention of a few newly mapped areas of Arkady's estate in *A Month in the Country* associates the idea of uncertainty and potential dispossession. Later in the scene Arkady realises how emotionally dispossessed he is, with his personal integrity in ruins: "I can't talk to you like this, Michel … Oh my God, have you any idea how destroyed I am?" (91).

The closing scene of Turgenev's *A Month in the Country* abounds in departures and Lizaveta Bogdanovna, who has the last words, refers to her going away too. The future holds a different, perhaps worse, though yet barely known fate for the characters. Friel must have felt some connection between this ending and the one in his *Dancing at Lughnasa*, where the family are still together but the unavoidably approaching rearrangement of their future lives is already known. The similarity becomes reinforced by Friel having Anna order Katya to serve coffee out on the lawn, where the sisters spread the tablecloth to have their tea at the end of *Dancing at Lughnasa*. Michael, the narrator utters the last words summarising his memories, stressing the capa-

---

[19] Brian Friel, *Fathers and Sons* (London: Faber and Faber, 1987), 44. All further references are to this edition.

[20] Cf. also Robert Tracy, op. cit. 22.

[21] Brian Friel, *Philadelphia, Here I Come! Selected Plays* (Washington, D. C.: The Catholic Univ. of America Press, 1984), 40.

bility of dance to express more than language can, while music accompanies the fading of the lights on the stage. One is left with a strong sense of the inevitability of fate but also of the never really graspable richness and mystery of human life. Friel's *A Month in the Country* closes also with music letting the feeling of melancholy and eternal sadness creep in too.

Several details and linguistic features of Friel's stage version of *Fathers and Sons* have their echoes in his other retranslation of Turgenev. Most worthy of mention is the servant figures having a greater role and far more emphasis on their individuality and problems than in Turgenev. As Richard York aptly observes, "Friel's vision is of a total society."[22] In his *A Month in the Country,* the central love story of infatuation and jealousies becomes parodied by the emotional entanglements of the lower class characters. In contrast with their frustrations, however, Katya's and Matvey's final reconciliation and happiness become fully emphasised. On the other hand, the figure of landlord Arkady Islayev in Friel's version resembles landlord Nikolai in *Fathers and Sons*. Busy and often confused, though for different reasons, both tend to grope for words and an understanding of the situation they find themselves in. In the crucial, respective dialogues of the young main heroes and the older main heroines in Friel the same phrase appears in different contexts. Anna Odintsov's blaming of Bazarov in *Fathers and Sons*, "You've misunderstood the whole situation. You've misread the whole thing" (54), recurs transformed into the infatuated Natalya's question of ambiguous self-doubt: "Are you saying I've misread the whole situation?" (70). The self-referential tinge of the wording corresponds to Friel's artistic conviction that reading and translation happen for the sake of the never complete act of understanding.

Michel Rakitin's leaving the family in Friel's version appears not unlike Bazarov's prolonged farewell in his *Fathers and Sons*, which is an addition to Turgenev. In both cases the action proceeds slowly and awkwardly, indicating people's preoccupation with what is of more immediate interest to themselves, to such an extent that the one who goes away hardly counts. The cacophony of voices makes the scene enormously comic in *A Month in the Country*:

MICHEL	If you'll excuse me—
ANNA	Natalya, Arkady.
ARKADY	Ah. She's gone to her room — to lie down.
LIZAVETA	(To Doctor) Go and have a look at her.
MICHEL	Goodbye, Herr Schaff.
SCHAFF	"'Bye? — 'bye?" — But I am not going nowhere!
DOCTOR	She's in her room now?
LIZAVETA	Is Vera with her?
ARKADY	Perhaps leave her for a while.

---

[22] Richard York, op. cit. 171.

ANNA	Was it some sort of weak turn?
ARKADY	I promise you — she's fine.
MICHEL	I'm about to leave, everybody.
ANNA	That little Katya exaggerates.
LIZAVETA	If I can be of any help?
SCHAFF	All day people tell me 'Bye — 'Bye — 'Bye.
ARKADY	Goodbye, Herr Schaff.
SCHAFF	But I am not exiting!
ARKADY	Ah. Splendid.
ANNA	That little maid's been behaving strangely all day.
MICHEL	I'm afraid I have to go — (105)

Michel's repeated attempts at saying farewell are neglected mainly because of Arkady's and his mother's concern for the absent Natalya's well-being. Ironically, the real reason for her misery remains unknown to them. The general lack of understanding and consideration manifests itself also in the fact that the interlocutors' sentences barely connect. The humour of the scene is largely enhanced by Schaff's, the German tutor's, misunderstandings and linguistic blunders which Friel makes ample use of during the whole play. Therefore Schaff has more of a role here than in Turgenev, and, though in comic colours, he shares a lot with the kind of outside commentators that the author often employs in his oeuvre, for instance in *Aristocrats*.

A Month in the Country fits in the sequence of Friel's mature works also because it draws attention to language and the problems of comprehension. Bolshintsov, for instance, desperately searches for words with which to approach Vera: "It's the words, Doctor, the words! What am I going to *say* to her? Because if I can't speak, how can I propose to her?" (51). His linguistic crisis derives from the general modern awareness of the world depending on the word. Among the foreign Schaff's ridiculous mistakes the very first one, where he wrongly uses "trumpery" when intending to say "trump" (17), has no basis in Turgenev's original. Appearing at the opening of Friel's version, its significance lies in preparing the audience for an unfolding conflict of meanings and values in the play itself.

Dialogue with Other Works

Jauss also discusses "an eventful history of literature," where "the next work can solve formal and moral problems left behind by the last work, and present new problems in turn."[23] Analogously, Friel's *A Month in the Country* highlights and explains some of the ideas of the original, in the course of reinterpreting its emotional confusion. In his introduction to his own translation of

---

[23] Hans Robert Jauss, op. cit. 32.

Turgenev's play, Richard Freeborn argues that it "is labelled a 'comedy' no doubt because it sets out to explore and illumine, in the subtlest and least didactic of ways, the absurdity of human passion" (XII). Besides staging the cavalcade of conflicting and uncontrollable feelings, Friel's play's comments on love add up to a more complex picture. It is the meaning of the so prodigally used word itself that he challenges, most notably when he has Vera argue for its renewal to Aleksey: "Esteem—affection—love; maybe you're right; maybe they are synonymous; maybe they should be. The fool, the loose-mouths talk only of 'love.' But maybe we should all settle for esteem—just a little esteem" (79). In Act Two Scene Two, the disappointed Michel cynically remarks to Aleksey that he sees love as a catastrophe and "An endless process of shame and desolation and despair when you are stripped—you strip yourself!—of every semblance of dignity and self-respect; when you grovel in the hope of a casual word or a sly smile or a secret squeeze of the hand" (94). So far not much breakaway from the original—but Friel does not let this remain without a counter-argument. His old lady, Anna, speaks about another kind of love, offered "without reservation" which, even though "neither fully appreciated nor fully reciprocated," makes fortunate those people who are capable of it (107). The ambiguity of this fortune, however, is revealed when she adds that such people do not usually believe themselves fortunate. Nevertheless, the audience may feel provoked to reconsider both Michel's and Anna's arguments in the context of his/her own experiences.

Friel's version also hints at a problem related to the "lived praxis" and "the background of the everyday experience of life"[24] in the last decade of the twentieth century. It is the awareness that power frequently proves unpredictable and is prone to irresponsible action, easily leading to both destructive and self-destructive results. In comparison with his source, Friel's play further emphasises the authority of Natalya, who frequently speaks, or is spoken of, using words and expressions with reference to her strength, most of the characters' fear of her and the fact that her commands have to be obeyed. In vain does Schaff, for instance, ask for her permission to visit his old mother. She wants to order people to stay or leave, freely claims how sick she is of all of them and calls Michel and Arkady lapdog and pup in turn, peremptorily adding that all decisions can be made only by herself. In spite of everything, she also manages to maintain her husband's need of her. It becomes deeply ironical that while she interferes in the life of others, ruins friendships and forces her dependents to choose self-hurting solutions, she remains unable to control herself. Colder and crueller than Turgenev's, Friel's Natalya seems, however, more vulnerable at the same time. While in the original play she expresses despair at being left by both Aleksey and Michel, Friel arranges her to

---

24 Ibid., 41.

break down in impotent rage and repeatedly underlines her selfishness at this point: "How dare he, the pup! ... And who is he to decide I haven't the courage to throw all this up and go with him! ... The bastard!" (102). The real problem, of course, lies in the fact that her own frustration and defenceless-ness entail unintended damage all around, thereby raising the issue of the rela-tion between power, self and others. In this respect, the play proves not only a version of Turgenev but also another expression of the "sense of dislocation between public definitions of the self ... and the actual life of the affections,"[25] present in almost all of Friel's dramatic work.

In parenthesis, Richard York's essay on Friel's *Three Sisters* and *Fathers and Sons* makes the remark that "despite the frequent use of twentieth century terms in the characters' speech" the "loyalty to the period setting" keeps up the dialogue, the tension between past and present. Then he poses the rhetorical question why exactly this is significant.[26] In *A Month in the Country* the fu-sion of a mid-nineteenth-century Russian story and late twentieth-century feelings and responses in a vibrant and disturbing way, carries a special force for the contemporary Irish and also non-Irish audience, in that it transmits one of their basic experiences. Living in the present, building up on what went be-fore, people cannot but have a constant sense of the past surrounding them, the frames of their lives being rooted in history, in an amalgamation of cultures. By means of all the above textual and structural alterations, this additional meaning of Friel's retranslation transcends but does not leave the world of the story and indirectly characterises its late twentieth century audience as well.

A Month in the Country has had many revivals on the English stages in the last couple of decades.[27] In 1994 the Albery Theatre ventured it with consid-erable success, using Richard Freeborn's translation. Compared with the pre-vious English translation, Isaiah Berlin's, this text appears modernised, more language-conscious and even bolder in its phrasing. Still following the origi-nal, though with some necessary cuts, like the simultaneously running one of Pesti Színház, Budapest, the Albery Theatre production did not step outside the play's admittedly rich possibilities. Sometimes, the action even conveyed a sense of the all too obvious. Of course Vera's gestures betrayed her, of course Natalya wore a dazzlingly red dress when filled with hope. It needs a free translation to offer something decidedly more. Having been rewritten from a text read in a specific way, Friel's version of Turgenev's *A Month in the*

---

25 Terence Brown, "'Have We a Context?': Transition, Self and Society in the Theatre of Brian Friel." Alan J. Peacock (ed.), op. cit. 191.

26 Richard York, op. cit. 166-67.

27 See April FitzLyon and Alexander Schouvaloff, Catalogue to an exhibition on *A Month in the Country* presented by the Theatre Museum in the Victoria and Albert Museum 1-31 May 1983.

Country reflects the processes of reception itself. Besides presenting the theatre with a highly appealing and digestible piece, with his unique method Friel exposes his audience to a complex dialogue between cultures, works, artists and themselves. He refashions also the Beckettian truth that it is the dialogue that keeps us here.

Brian Friel and American Drama

Background

During their first tour of the United States in 1911, the Abbey Players presented works by Synge, Yeats, Augusta Gregory, T. C. Murray and Lennox Robinson. A young man in the audience, the Irish-American Eugene O'Neill, attended these performances with great enthusiasm and started his own playwriting career inspired by Irish drama. Synge's influence on his early period can be seen in the field of "theme, treatment, mood and motif" as Péter Egri has pointed out.[1] Early in his career Irish playwright Brian Friel (1929-) spent several months of 1963 in Minneapolis, Minnesota, observing director Tyrone Gutherie at work and becoming acquainted with American theatre in general there. Following this experience he wrote:

> ... those months in America gave me a sense of liberation—remember this was my first parole from inbred claustrophobic Ireland—and that sense of liberation conferred on me a valuable self-confidence and a necessary perspective so that the first play I wrote immediately after I came home, *Philadelphia, Here I Come!* was a lot more assured than anything I had attempted before.[2]

Although it would be risky to assert that American drama has exerted influence on Friel's oeuvre, some parallels are hard to overlook.

In the 1950-60s Arthur Miller's *Death of a Salesman* was so ubiquitously present on the English-speaking stage that certain themes and motifs of this masterpiece crop up in Irish works as well. Thomas Murphy's *A Whistle in the Dark*, first performed in 1961, depicts a self-deceiving father and his sons, the eldest of whom makes desperate efforts to free himself from the father's influence. Although in Murphy's play the source and unfolding of tragedy differ from what *Death of a Salesman* (1949) presents, the concern with identity is recognizable in both. In *A Whistle in the Dark* the father is remembered to have once stolen a coat that he did not need at all from the golf club, and to have thrown it over a wall in frustrated revenge on the more lucky and prosperous. The motif is reminiscent of Biff's theft of the millionaire, Oliver's, valuable pen, an act being equally meaningless. An early, now "disowned" play

---

[1] Péter Egri, "Synge and O'Neill: Inspiration and Influence." Wolfgang Zach, Heinz Kosok (eds.), *Literary Interrelations: Ireland, England and the World 2. Comparison and Impact* (Tübingen: Günter Narr Verlag, 1987), 261-68.
[2] Brian Friel, *Self-Portrait,* qtd. in: Ulf Dantanus, *Brian Friel, A Study* (London: Faber and Faber, 1988), 51

of Friel from 1959 bears the title *A Doubtful Paradise*. Its protagonist, Willie Logue proves a relative of Willie Loman, not only on account of his name, but also because "his life falls into the focus of his self-deception."[3] At the same time, Friel started his playwriting career showing great sensitivity to the problems of the Catholic community in Derry, similarly to Miller's consciousness of social issues. According to Christopher Murray, Miller can be mentioned "in the catalogue of possible influences" on the work of Friel.[4]

Inside Their Heads

Philadelphia, first performed in 1964, divides its protagonist, the 25 year-old Gar O'Donnell into a private self and a public self, played by two actors on stage. Many critics have found the device similar to O'Neill's *Day's Without End* (1934), where the protagonist is represented by two figures, John and Loving, and the latter's face is a mask. Friel, however, denied any knowledge of that play before writing his *Philadelphia*.[5] By having the much louder Private Gar beside Public Gar his aim was to reveal not only the outer side of the young man but also his thoughts, the deeper layers of his mind that are not available for others. The dramatization of the inner life of one particular character while the others are seen from the outside only, establishes his/her limited point of view in the work.[6]

Friel acquaints his audience with Gar's aspirations, dreams and fears by making his inner side seen and heard. The play premièred at the Gate Theatre in Dublin, where Alpho O'Reilly designed the set in a way that instead of Friel's originally planned scenes "the whole should be seen together, rather in the mode of Arthur Miller; so he cut the house in half and revealed its internal ramification, upstairs and down."[7] O'Reilly rightly felt a parallel with *Death of a Salesman*, originally titled *The Inside of His Head*, where the flashbacks have a great "psychological complexity, for what is revealed is not simply the memory of an earlier event but a new experience, a fusion of past and present."[8] At several points in the play Willy Loman's mind begins to wander toward past events mingled with their painful implications for him in the present. The audience tends to form a picture of the major issues filtered through Willy because, due to Miller's method, his point of view dominates the play.

---

[3] Desmond Maxwell, "'Figures in a Peepshow': Friel and the Irish Dramatic Tradition." Alan Peacock (ed.), *The Achievement of Brian Friel* (Gerrards Cross: Colin Smythe, 1993), 52.

[4] Christopher Murray, "Friel's 'Emblems of Adversity' and the Yeatsian Example." Ibid., 69.

[5] Cf. Anthony Roche, *Contemporary Irish Drama* (Dublin: Gill and Macmillan, 1994), 79.

[6] See Edward Groff, "Point of View in Modern Drama." *Modern Drama,* Dec., 1959, 270.

[7] Christopher Fitz-Simon, *The Boys: A Biography of Micheál MacLiammoir and Hilton Edwards* (London: Nick Hern Books, 1994), 276.

[8] Edward Groff, op. cit. 275.

After the humiliation of waiting for the millionaire in vain, Willy's elder son, Biff, demonstrates a marked change in his overall attitude. He expresses his realization that both of them have been struggling with identity problems. At the end more emphasis shifts to Biff and his realistic self-awakening, which underscores Willy's lifelong self-deception:

> BIFF   I am not a leader of men, Willy, and neither are you. You were never anything but a hard-working drummer who landed in the ash-can like all the rest of them! I'm one dollar an hour, Willy! ... I'm not bringing home any prizes any more, and you're going to stop waiting for me to bring them home![9]

In Friel's *Philadelphia* the dominant point of view is also somewhat challenged by the other major character, Gar's father at the end of the drama. The old man has been monosyllabic and extremely reserved till then; one could even feel a lack of concern on his part for his son who is planning to emigrate to Philadelphia in the morning. The flashbacks in the play show only Gar's memories of his past life in Ballybeg. In the final scene he makes a desperate effort to capture his father's attention by recounting a childhood memory about the two of them fishing together, sailing in a blue boat. Gar's father recollects something too, though his story contains very different elements. Gradually his feelings and doubts about a lonely future become articulated. Looking inside the father this way throws an additional light on Gar, suggesting that the younger man is surely not the sole sufferer and victim in the microcosm of Ballybeg, and "the play is tilted towards a more objective, broader perspective."[10] The essential resemblance between father and son is underlined by Madge: "When the boss was his (GAR's) age, he was the very same as him: leppin, and eejitin' about and actin' the clown; as like as two peas. And when he's (GAR) the age the boss is now, he'll turn out just the same."[11] The use of a dominant point of view in drama, exemplified by *Salesman* and *Philadelphia*, proves an excellent vehicle to portray the inside of a character's head. Nevertheless, the resulting restrictedness calls for testing it against another consciousness in order to draw a fuller picture.

---

[9] Arthur Miller, *Death of a Salesman* (Harmondsworth: Penguin Books, 1962), 105.

[10] Anthony Roche, op. cit. 101.

[11] Brian Friel, *Philadelphia, Here I Come! Selected Plays* (Washington D.C.: The Catholic Univ. of America Press, 1984), 98.

Self-reflection and Versions of Reality

Most of Friel's later plays are interwoven with different approaches to and conflicting interpretations of events and experiences from *The Freedom of the City* (1973) to *Molly Sweeney* (1994). His frequent implementation of techniques of distancing and self-reflection has been "attentive to the development of modern European and American theatre."[12] In *Living Quarters* (1977) he uses a unique dramatic figure, called Sir, who is neither a narrator nor a mere commentator, but a combination of the two and a great deal more. An American parallel can be seen in the Stage Manager of Thornton Wilder's *Our Town* (1938), who introduces, interrupts and intrudes into the action and then closes the whole. Both appear as kind of directors of the respective plays, fulfilling a complex role to build up a distancing effect "which emphasize(s) the fact that the drama is at one level a contrivance — a matter of selecting, condensing and aesthetically ordering depicted human experience."[13] Wilder's Stage Manager and Friel's Sir are voices of Fate at the same time, in their own fashion. The former with his suprahuman power, the latter with his ledger containing the account of past events as they live in the minds of those who took part in them. Through this device, in both cases there is "the presence of a formidable auctorial mind"[14] which makes the plays intellectual and geared toward the unfolding of an idea. In *Our Town* that central experience is describable as "the pathos of the great commonplaces of human life, birth, marriage and death."[15]

While admittedly a product of the other characters' imaginations, Friel's Sir embodies how imagination, as an authority, can become master of man. What the ledger contains passes for the reality of the unalterable past, accepted as such by those who have, in their separate collectivity, created it all. Nevertheless, the characters tend to wish to change the fixed script in the reliving situation which makes up the play itself. According to Sir,

> ... out of some deep psychic necessity, they have conceived me—the ultimate arbiter, the powerful and impartial referee, the final abjucator, a kind of human Hansard who knows those tiny little details and interprets them accurately. And yet no sooner do they conceive me with my authority and my

---

[12] Terence Brown, *Ireland. A Social and Cultural History 1922-1985* (London: Fontana Press, 1990), 319-20.

[13] Alan Peacock, "Translating the Past: Friel, Greece and Rome." Alan Peacock (ed.), op. cit. 117-18.

[14] Thomas Kilroy, "Theatrical Text and Literary Text." Ibid., 94.

[15] Francis Fergusson, *The Human Image in Dramatic Lierature* (New York: Doubleday Anchor Books, 1957), 55.

knowledge than they begin flirting with the idea of circumventing me, of foxing me, of outwitting me. Curious, isn't it?[16]

Our Town lacks this (postmodern?) interplay between reality and imagination, but is unmistakably American in portraying small-town life in New England. At times even a touch of satire manifests itself, for example in Mr. Webb's negative answer to the question whether there is "any culture or love of beauty in Grover's Corners": "Well, ma'am, there ain't much—not in the sense you mean."[17]

The way individual characters in *Living Quarters* rebel against the course of events or question their authority allows us to see their most obsessive private features, which in turn is relevant to the Irish in general. The local Chaplin, for one, betrays insecurity of identity. Anna, the Irish Phaedra of the play subtitled "after Hippolytus," seems tortured by the moral burden of her infidelity and impatiently tries to get her confession over. Her cuckolded husband, Commandant Frank Butler, on the other hand, self-pityingly harps on the depth of injustice and the wounds he has had to suffer.

The individuals' inclination to forge their own versions of reality appears more emphatically in Friel's *Faith Healer* (1979), a play based on the Irish storytelling tradition. In the monologues of its three characters, Frank, Grace and Teddy, the shared past is fictionalized in different ways, making reality private without one unchallengable version. A similar tendency can be identified in the second part of Arthur Miller's career. In *The Price* (1968) the two brothers, Victor and Walter, cultivate diverging memories and opinions of their relationship with their father as well as their own decisive choices in life. Walter's remark sounds rather revealing: "We invent ourselves, Vic, to wipe out what we know. You invent a life of self-sacrifice, a life of duty; but what never existed here cannot be upheld."[18] Friel's technique of separated monologues intensifies the characters' inventing and fictionalizing not only themselves but each other. At the end of her speech Grace claims to be but one of the fictions of her husband.

Faith Healer leaves ambiguity behind, as it has touched the core of human experience, the desire to shake off the doubts, suspense and fear that constitute existence. Impending death through self-sacrifice brings relief to Frank: "Then for the first time there was no atrophying terror; and the maddening questions were silent."[19] Of *The Price,* its author said: "… *The Price* is about—the tension…. The satisfaction is the perception of the tension. 'Cause it is not solved,

16 Brian Friel, Living Quarters. *Selected Plays*, 177-78.
17 Thornton Wilder, *Our Town* (Harmondsworth: Penguin Books, 1967), 36.
18 Arthur Miller, *The Price* (Harmondsworth: Penguin Books, 1970), 90.
19 Brian Friel, *Faith Healer. Selected Plays*, 376. All further references are to this edition.

and life isn't. It can't be solved."[20] At the end of the play old Solomon, who has observed the verbal fight of the other two from a distance, remains alone and starts listening to the Laughing Record on the phonograph. In Friel's play Teddy, the outsider and survivor, puts on his record at the end of the third monologue. These gestures suggest continuity, the larger realm of life lying beyond the individuals' misgivings and struggle for meaning.

Fables and Parables

The first monograph on Friel mentions the indirect influence of Edward Albee, although without giving an example.[21] One particular motif, however, characteristically crops up in the work of both dramatists, namely stories about animals which throw more light on some of the crucial aspects of their plays. Albee's shaggy dog tale, an uncommonly long inbedded story within the larger one about Jerry's life in *The Zoo Story* (1958) is a shocking allegory of misunderstanding, failure of communication and resulting indifference. In fact, it mirrors the central crisis of the play itself. Friel's *Faith Healer* is a complex of stories with a great range of minor stories in them. Teddy's monologue contains "shaggy dog allegories that reflect back on his relationship with Frank and Grace."[22] In contrast with Albee, Friel's animal story is both amusing and fantastic. The two dogs Teddy claims to have had once differed in talent and ambition: the female brilliant at everyday chores but no performer, while the male, a whippet, a sensational genius in front of an audience but "subnormal" in other ways. Frank and Grace srike one much like this, different and also complementary.

Friel's *Molly Sweeney* (1994) is also built out of the monologues of three characters. The central one, the initially blind Molly, possesses an inner sight and highly developed senses using which she makes a world for herself devoid of self-pity and resignation. After having both eyes operated on, the abundance of visual sensations conveying reality in all its harshness to her proves too unhospitable and alarming. From the growing dizziness of partial sight she withdraws into private fantasy, peopled with ghosts and visions. One of her adventure-loving husband, Frank's stories sounds like an ironical parallel to her case, in that it also depicts shrinking back from the untravelled and instinctively returning to the familiar:

---

[20] "Appendix: A Conversation with Arthur Miller." Leonard Moss, *Arthur Miller* (Boston: Twayne Publishers, 1980), 121.
[21] D. E. S. Maxwell, *Brian Friel* (Lewisburg: Bucknell Univ. Press, 1973), 109.
[22] Anthony Roche, op. cit. 123.

Billy Hughes and his crazy scheme. He had heard that there was a pair of badgers in a sett at the edge of the lake. When Anna was flooded in three weeks time, they would be drowned. They would have to be moved. Would I help him? ... the moment we cut them out of the nets and tried to push them down the new whole, well naturally they went blind ... And where did they head for? Of course—of course—straight back to the old sett at the edge of the water—the one we destroyed with all our digging! Well, what could you do but laugh?[23]

The badgers go blind when they are forced out of their natural environment, and Molly cannot adapt to the fundamental change the eye-operations involve, partial sight bringing greater blindness for her. She lands feeling at home only in a "borderline country," where the real and imagined mingle and are accepted together, unquestioned.

Jerry's darkly grotesque, shocking story in Albee's play is narrated as parable "for the benefit of Peter" and as "the means whereby he arrives at the meaning of his own experiences."[24] In *Faith Healer* and *Molly Sweeney*, narrated by stage Englishman and stage Irishman figures, the comic animal stories reinforce the plays' themes with an ironic effect. As both Albee and Friel are known to have been influenced by Beckett, the source might be common, in spite of apparent differences. In the middle of *Waiting for Godot* Vladimir sings about a dog whose story returns to its beginning like the whole play itself does.

Faith Healers

Seven decades before Friel's *Faith Healer*, which premièred on Broadway, American poet-playwright William Vaughn Moody wrote *The Faith Healer* (1909), his most successful play that Friel may or may not have known about when conceiving his. Moody's main character, Michaelis also practises faith healing, and the play begins following his arrival at the home of the Beeler family. After wandering from place to place healing people with varying success, he realizes that the covered route makes the shape of a cross on the map. In Friel's play Frank Hardy's incantation of the names of Welsh and Scottish villages gives the audience a sense of place, that of the Celtic fringe. In contrast with the religious implication of Michaelis's cross-shaped itinerary, the chain of place-names used by Friel draws on ancient Irish lore. For both faith

---

[23] Brian Friel, *Molly Sweeney* (Loughcrew Oldcastle: The Gallery Press, 1994), 60-61. All further references are to this edition.

[24] C. W. E. Bigsby, *Modern American Drama 1945-1990* (Cambridge: Cambridge Univ. Press, 1992), 132.

healers, it is the completion of their long journeys that involves the real and decisive test: their power is needed to cure an invalid in a wheelchair.

Having been conceived in two eras and cultures widely apart, Moody's and Friel's faith healers differ considerably in their characters and aims. Michaelis is fulfilling a mission; he has been given power by God to do good to mankind after years of preparation in the mountains. He is a Christ-like figure who relates having heard a voice sending him forth to begin to heal the sufferers. Subsequently he raised a young Mexican boy from his grave as his first miraculous act:

> Just before daylight, when the other watchers were asleep, the power of the spirit came strong upon me. I bowed myself upon the boy's body, and prayed. My heart burned within me, for I felt his heart begin to beat! His eyes opened. I told him to arise, and he arose. He that was dead arose and was alive again![25]

Friel's Frank Hardy bears pagan characteristics, which description is supported by the reference to the ritual of his final sacrifice as a "Dionysian night. A Bacchanalian night" (340). In his healing activity no sign of altruism or sense of mission manifests itself, but it proves a series of attempts at self-healing, the power coming from God knows where:

> ... when I stood before a man and placed my hands on him and watched him become whole in my presence, those were nights of exultation, of consummation—no, not that I was doing good, giving relief, spreading joy—good God, no, nothing at all to do with that; but because the questions that undermined my life then became meaningless and because I knew that for those few hours I had become whole in myself, and perfect in myself ... (333)

Frank Hardy's personality and "craft" are seen in a most complex way. The fact that he sets up one-night performances places him in the role of the artist, whose talent remains a mystery for both himself and others. He is an artist in the ancient sense, relying on the magic of words, a Druid fulfilling the priest's functions as well. The pagan side, however, becomes fused with the Christian element reflecting the texture of modern Irish culture. Described in Teddy's monologue, Frank's most memorable success took place in the old Methodist church of a Welsh village, where he cured "every single person" out of the ten coming to the performance. The actual healing sounds more significant in spiritual than in physical terms: "Hardly a word was spoken. It was like as if

---

[25] William Vaughn Moody, *The Faith Healer. The Poems and Plays of William Vaughn Moody Vol. II* (Cambridge: The Riverside Press, 1912), 211. All further references are to this edition.

not only had he taken away whatever it was was wrong with them, but like he had given them some great content in themselves as well" (359). Frank utters his last words in the final monologue of the play with his hat taken off "as if he were entering a church" (376). The device of presenting his story in the different versions of four monologues, not unlike Christ's in the Gospels,[26] also reinforces the Christian parallel. According to Matthew, the Messiah crossed the sea to come to his own land where "they brought to him a paralytic, lying on his bed" (Matthew 8. 9) whose sins he forgave and whose body he cured. Confronted with a task of similar magnitude on his homecoming to Ireland, Frank fails: the human being can aspire to the unlimited power of God but cannot achieve it.

In Moody's play the faith with which Michaelis is healing other people remains dominantly connected with Christianity and religion. The play is, however, not without a shade of the more ancient and pagan aspects of human culture. A picture from the supplement of the Sunday paper is pinned on a wall in the Beelers' home, entitled "Pan and the Pilgrim." It shows a forest meeting between the Pilgrim, the representative of Christian belief, and the nature god, Pan. The latter's pipe pouring forth an enchanting tune seems to influence the Christian wanderer. On the other hand, the meeting of these two figures foreshadows what will happen to Michaelis, the faith healer. He starts losing his power earned from God when he finds himself in earthly love with Rhoda, the Beelers' niece. Nature and faith appear incompatible: Michaelis's rapidly waning power is demonstrated by the fact that the invalid, Mrs. Beeler, whom he rendered able to walk earlier, sinks back into her wheelchair powerless. The healer's situation turns critical as there waits a crowd outside to be cured, and disappointing them would involve a fate similar to that of Frank Hardy, whose inability to cure the invalid McGarvey is suggested to have resulted in his assassination.

Moody's play, however, provides a turning point which renews the healing belief, and brings triumph over the coldness of scientific facts. The beloved Rhoda confesses to be wounded in her soul and in need of becoming healed through refilling her with faith and trust. To carry out this task the power of Michaelis returns, and love and faith form a harmonious union promising happiness as well as Christian work for others. At the same time Michaelis gains spiritual and moral victory over the heartless and faithless physician, Rhoda's former lover, who considered her as a mere object and plaything. *The Faith Healer* ends on the note of idealistic faith in good capable of winning and healing power restorable through love, by "the mystery that is man, and the mercy that is God" (334). On Easter morning, when the action closes, the sick

---

[26] A student, Bernadette Pálfai has called my attention to this detail during a seminar.

baby whom Michaelis failed to cure earlier, is discovered resurrecting from its death-like, hopeless state.

In the postmodern era there is hardly any space for such unambiguity. Grace's need of Frank cannot prevent the tragic outcome. When Frank feels that things have been "lean for a long time" (338), the three of them return to Ireland. This homecoming confronts him with the kind of sickness against which he is powerless. However, Friel's Irish world is not entirely devoid of hope either. Frank's Dionysian death, a sacrifice at harvest time with a wedding celebration in the background, promises renewal. In the words of Anthony Roche,

> He (Frank) is not only the sacrifical scapegoat for a community's inherited ills, as Christy Mahon was before him; but the play's closing act, which is both an act of destruction (annihilation) and re-creation from nothing, is one rife with possibilities for a new post-colonial identity and drama.[27]

Moody uses conventional dramatic form, Biblical allusions and a large cast to convince his audience of the renewed force of faith in the modern world. The name of Michealis recalls archangel Micheal in the Bible, who successfully contends with the devil. *The Faith Healer* offers a Christian version of faith healing and self-sacrifice to revitalize belief in turn-of-the-century America. Friel's *Faith Healer* qualifies as a largely pagan version that ends with the violent sacrifice of the Dionysian healer in a community where everything points to the deepest, sorest layers of the past. Frank Hardy's name carries the tone of sincerity and difficulty.

Memory Plays

Next, Tennessee Williams's dramatizing memory into play is worth comparing with aspects in the work of Friel. As Fintan O'Toole succinctly summarizes,

> The connections between *[Dancing at] Lughnasa* and *The Glass Managerie* are reasonably obvious ones. The use of the narrator as a device for the suspension and conflation of time, the elegiac tone of the narration, the use of a mentally disturbed young woman (Laura, Rose) whose sexuality takes on a critical edge, the guilty departure of the narrator, the sense of a family trapped as an anachronism in an increasingly hostile world, the persistence of old ceremonies, and, above all, perhaps, the use of music, all link the plays together.[28]

---

[27] Anthony Roche, op. cit. 121.

[28] Fintan O'Toole, "Marking Time: From *Making History* to *Dancing at Lughnasa*." Alan Peacock (ed.), op. cit. 209.

It may be more than an interesting coincidence that the two plays were running at the Abbey Theatre during the same period in 1990.[29] Both plays take place in the 1930s when Ireland and the American South were entering a new phase of their development, toward modernization. "Williams pictures a society on the turn. Not for nothing was Chekhov his favourite playwright."[30] These words of C. W. E. Bigsby are equally true of Brian Friel, who even re-translated/adapted two great Russian predecessors, Turgenev and Chekhov.

In both *Lughnasa* and *The Glass Menagerie* there widens a gap between the individuals and the community they belong to. The Mundy girls created by Friel live isolated and cannot take part in the harvest festival because their Christian way of life is no longer reconcilable with pagan practices. To compensate for this loss, dance is central to *Lughnasa* as a release of energy as well as a language beyond words, with which the most personal experience can be articulated and the harmony between body and soul restored. In *The Glass Managerie* the women do not have company and friends, and Tom knows little about the people he meets day by day at the warehouse. Laura lives in her private dream world, among her fragile glass figures. Her dancing with the Irish-American Jim means also a temporary stepping out of the usual limitations her life and personality impose on her, but the venture ends in frustration and disappointment. Before she blows out the candles to end the play, her mother is said to be comforting her with "slow and graceful, almost dancelike"[31] gestures.

Both Laura and the sisters in Friel's play face loneliness and corresponding lack of prospects in a changing world. The act of dancing in *Lughnasa*, however, is more liberating because more universal and Dionysian, similar to Zarathustra's dance of life, and the play opens up toward a broader vista. Laura's glass unicorn, the breaking of which symbolizes the loss of illusions, has an earthy, comic parallel in the single-horned, winking brown cow of Gerry's story, walking on the road to Ballybeg in *Lughnasa*. The brown cow is a traditional symbol of Ireland, whose fantastic features added here may suggest the grotesque transformations of the Irish society.

The memory technique does not work in the same way in *The Glass Menagerie* and *Lughnasa*. In the former play, Tom, the narrator, is one of the protagonists; he enters the stage and takes part in the events of the recalled past. Therefore all seems real and convincing about the family's decline and Tom's subsequent pangs of conscience. Michael, the narrator of *Lughnasa*,

---

[29] Richard Pine, David Grant and Derek West, "Brian Friel's New Play for the Abbey." *Theatre Ireland* Spring 1990, 7.

[30] C. W. E. Bigsby, op. cit. 43.

[31] Tennessee Williams, *The Glass Menagerie*. George McMichael (gen. ed.), *Anthology of American Literature Vol. II* (New York: Macmillan, 1985), 1646.

does not transform into his younger self to accompany his sisters, although they take him to be there. This creates a larger distance between past and present, and there asserts itself a greater ambiguity about what is real or imagined than in Williams's play. Michael's first monologue reports "some awareness of a widening breach between what seemed to be and what was,"[32] introducing a dream-like atmosphere. The play, however, closes with Michael's allusions to one haunting memory, in which the "actual and illusory" mingle and "everybody seems to be floating on ... sweet sounds" (71). The memory dissolves in dancing itself, the ritual, wordless ceremony that connects past, present and future and transcends individual tragedies.

Parallel Changes

Arthur Miller, rather exceptionally compared with his whole oeuvre, included a timid and embittered woman's dance in his 1993 play, *The Last Yankee*. The ageing Karen's pathetic tap-dancing in a ridiculous outfit is a climactic point of the work in that it involves a test for all the four characters to accept or reject her thus articulated wish for individual freedom and self-expression. Her unfolding performance proves too much to bear for her convention-bound husband whose outburst into furious shouts brings back a look of fear to Karen's face and the dance comes to an abrupt end. According to Nada Zeineddine, it was not until the later phase of his career that Miller gave a greater role to women in his plays.[33] The change was marked by *Elegy for a Young Lady* (1980) and *Playing for Time* (1981), in which women are connected with suffering and art. Placing a large amount of emphasis on women figures, *The Last Yankee* is also very much a play of women, where artistic activity appears as an escape from the world of maddening routines.

In his study of the contemporary Irish theatre, Anthony Roche discovers the "development of a more woman-centered drama ... anticipated by Samuel Beckett in some of his most important later plays."[34] Such examples in Beckett's oeuvre range from *Happy Days* (1961) to *Rockaby* (1980) through *Not I* (1972) and *Footfalls* (1975). It is a tendency Roche sees in Irish drama growing up beside the other significant tendency marked by moving "away from the idea of a single leading man and towards the sharing of the stage space between two male protagonists, neither of whom predominates."[35] Later

---

[32] Brian Friel, *Dancing at Lughnasa* (London: Faber and Faber, 1990), 2. All further references are to this edition.
[33] Nada Zeineddine, Because It Is My Name. *Problems of Identity Experienced by Women, Artists and Breadwinners in the Plays of Henrik Ibsen, Tennessee Williams and Arthur Miller* (Braunston Devon: Merlin Books Ltd., 1991), 209.
[34] Anthony Roche, op. cit. 283.
[35] Ibid., 79.

in their careers some other dramatists' turning to women characters is well observable too, both in Ireland and in America. Beside Miller's example one finds that of Albee who, three decades after his two-male *The Zoo Story* produced a virtually all-female play entitled *Three Tall Women*, first performed in 1991.

In the first part of Friel's career there is a dominance of male protagonists, although women lend memorable colours to the plays as well. *Philadelphia* rests on the male pair of Private Gar and Public Gar. *Making History* (1988) focuses on debates between the last Gaelic chieftain, Hugh O'Neill, and Lombard, the historian, about how to present and interpret the past. Two years later, *Lughnasa* entered the stage as Friel's first women's play par excellence. As discussed above, the technique employed in *Faith Healer*, where the figure of Frank Hardy is dominant, re-occurs in *Molly Sweeney*, but now centering on a woman. The number of the protagonists remains the same, two men and a woman, but the rearrangement of emphasis is unmistakable. Frank Hardy is a portrait of the artist as faith-healer and self-healer. Molly's story addresses seeing in the broadest possible sense and the wish for and ways of making one's own reality.

In Thomas Murphy's dramatic oeuvre the move from male-centeredness to female-plays is even more conspicuously marked. *The Sanctuary Lamp* (1975) and *The Gigli Concert* (1983) use two men and a woman, the latter playing secondary roles while the former work out their ways to reconciliation and self-realization, respectively. *Bailegangaire* from 1985, however, has three women characters and no males. Compared with the former two where tension becomes released, in the women's play Murphy achieves even more: a sense of homecoming and a new beginning.

Can there be a deeper reason for this non-negligible pattern of switching from male to female worlds in the drama of exclusively male authors? The following is a tentative hypothesis. Friel's male protagonists tend to wrestle with particular constraints and choices, as in *The Enemy Within* (1962), *Philadelphia, Faith Healer* and *Making History*. They are bound to be connected with particular activities and fields like spiritual life, healing, writing, assessing the past, politics and historiography. American parallels can be seen in *The Price* and several of Sam Shepard's and David Mamet's works. The women characters of the later Frielean plays, on the other hand, are more likely to embody general and universal concerns. The Mundy sisters in *Lughnasa* dance over the gap between drab reality and suppressed desire. Molly Sweeney faces the great test of life: to accept an imposed and fragmented existence or to go back to the privately developed—she does the latter. In the American arena, Albee's *Three Tall Women* brings together the major cycles of life itself in the three women who represent one and the same person at different ages.

Conclusion

The present inquiry leads to the conclusion that there are many bridges resting on the use of similar themes, motifs and techniques between the historically and culturally related national theatres of Ireland and America. A view of them as comparative study, however, necessarily identifies dissimilarities as well. Significant American drama was born in an independent country, while Irish drama emerged as part of a colonial culture. The former always remains closer to facts and contains at least a shade of pragmatism. Even when uncertainty dominates the American dramatic characters' worlds, they strive toward less ambiguity and discrimination. On the other hand, the century-old blurring of reality and imagination has left its mark on the drama of Ireland. Irish people have counterbalanced the painful and unbearable pressures of the (post)colonial situation with their own dreams and stories. Fact, fiction and myth often continue to permeate each other in the contemporary playwrights' works as well. For Friel this heritage seems to be a blessing and a burden at the same time, and he dramatizes their interrelations in a great variety of contexts. Making stories does not really help Gar among the deprivations of Ballybeg in *Philadelphia*. In *The Freedom of the City* (1973) and *Making History* fictions under various banners overshadow private truth. *Faith Healer* blends reality and fiction with exceptional originality, becoming Friel's "most Irish" play.[36] The painful necessity to come to terms with facts becomes an issue in *Aristocrats* (1979) and *Translations* (1980). After following the uncertainties of sight, *Molly Sweeney* ends in ambiguity accepted, a possible *ars poetica*:

> It certainly doesn't worry me anymore that what I think I see may be fantasy or indeed what I take to be imagined may very well be real—what's Frank's term?—external reality. Real—imagined—fact—fiction—fantasy—reality—there it seems to be. And it seems to be alright. And why should I question any of it anymore? (67)

---

[36] Ulf Dantanus, op. cit. 172.